Jo Seagar

The Cook School Recipes

Jo Seagar

The Cook School Recipes

photography by Jae Frew

RANDOM HOUSE
NEW ZEALAND

A RANDOM HOUSE BOOK published by Random House New Zealand
18 Poland Road, Glenfield, Auckland, New Zealand

A catalogue record for this book is available from the National Library of New Zealand

Random House International, Random House, 20 Vauxhall Bridge Road, London, SW1V 2SA, United
Kingdom; **Random House Australia Pty Ltd**, Level 3, 100 Pacific Highway, North Sydney 2060, Australia;
Random House South Africa Pty Ltd, Isle of Houghton, Corner Boundary Road and Carse O'Gowrie,
Houghton 2198, South Africa; **Random House Publishers India Private Ltd**, 301 World Trade Tower, Hotel
Intercontinental Grand Complex, Barakhamba Lane, New Delhi 110 001, India

First published 2008. Reprinted 2010, 2011.

© 2008 text, Jo Seagar; photographs, Jae Frew

The moral rights of the author have been asserted

ISBN 978 1 86941 972 1

Design: Kate Barraclough
Printed in China by Everbest Printing Co Ltd

Dedication

To our wonderful team at Seagars in Oxford: Phil Keen, Barnaby Wylie, Deborah O'Neill, Lyn Hunter and all the staff who have taken such pride in our cook school, café and kitchenware store. Each of you helps make it the big success it is. My special love and thanks to you all.

Thanks also to Jae Frew for the beautiful photography. You are such a wonderful friend and so creative and pleasant to work with. And thanks go to Jenny Hellen at Random House, Rachel Goodchild and Fiona McRae for wise counsel and editing. Thank you to Annie Graham, for her help with the photography and props. Also thanks to my good mate Maree O'Neill, for her hair and make-up skills — she's always there for me.

Special mention must go to Ross the fireman, the husband and wonderful partner, my friend, general dogsbody and a pretty good typist to boot. With love and thanks,

Jo

Contents

Introduction

I'd had a vision for a very long time of a country cook school, complete with an Aga oven, a small kitchen store and a simple café serving the kind of food people love to eat. Finding Oxford was like coming home — for us it has a sense of being in the right place at the right time.

People ask us, 'Why did you choose Oxford?' The answer is that Oxford chose the Seagars. Ross and I felt instantly comfortable here. The town was extremely welcoming and so we started a new phase in our lives.

Our original idea was to do fewer things better. In fact, we have never worked quite so hard in our lives, but it is all so terribly satisfying and rewarding that it doesn't all feel like work! We knew we had a winning idea, but nothing could have prepared us for the success of the whole venture. We touch wood and hope things will always be this good.

The cook school is my real passion. I so enjoy meeting each new class and seeing some of the same people return again and again, hungry for more. Time is a precious commodity these days, but it's not something you can put on your shopping list. However, at the cook school we are quick to use and pass on all the shortcuts we know — cheats' tips and user-friendly ingredients.

When you are entertaining, make it easy: keep the food part of your life uncomplicated. Cooking for those you love isn't meant to be the complete measure of your soul's worth to the planet. Our philosophy is about cooking intuitively and cooking from the heart. I love the praise, but I'm not prepared to slave away for days to achieve it, nor will I lay down my life for the cause. I'd much rather be out riding the range than be at home cooking on it.

It doesn't matter how good a cook you are, we all need some inspiration from time to time; that's what we aim to give you at the cook school and with this collection of new recipes from the school.

Here are some healthy ways to cook old, easy favourites and some inspirational new ideas. They're achievable after a busy working day and will easily satisfy not only your appetite but your creative side, too — there's something for the butcher, the baker and the cake decorator in all of you.

Familiarity with food is crucial. Even the phrase 'comfort food' is reassuring; nobody craves fusion extravaganzas! There is an essential wholesomeness to comfort food that is reminiscent of tea and toast on rainy afternoons. Getting together around a table to share a meal builds friendships and knits families together — there is so much more to it than just body fuel. My wish is that once you've tried these recipes you will want to incorporate them into your own repertoire for entertaining and sharing with friends and family.

Please enjoy!

Jo's mum Fay in the garden

Fay waiting on the steps

Jo and brother Guy

Jo decided to cut her own hair

Fay graduating from law school

Love that hat

Jo's parents, Fay and Martyn, on their wedding day

1. Nibbly Bits

Although time is the most luxurious commodity, it's not something you can put on your shopping list. Taking the time to have a few drinks and nibbles with friends and family can fill you up with love and laughter and fun. And sometimes, that is all you really need.

Brie and Pepperdew Bites

Pepperdews are small red capsicums that are pickled in brine. They are available in delis and good supermarkets.

Makes 48

4 sheets frozen flaky pastry, thawed
1 cup pepperdews, drained
125 g Brie (1 small round)
½ cup grated tasty cheese
3 eggs
1 cup cream
½ teaspoon salt
½ teaspoon freshly ground black pepper
2 tablespoons chopped parsley

Preheat the oven to 180°C. Spray 2 x 24-cup mini-muffin or tartlet tins with baking spray.

Cut out 5–6 cm circles of pastry and press into the tins. Chill for 10 minutes. Cut up the pepperdews and Brie so you have 48 pieces of each — enough for each lined tartlet tin. Place a piece of pepperdew, a piece of Brie and a sprinkling of grated cheese in each pastry shell.

Whisk the eggs, cream, salt, pepper and parsley together and, using a small jug, pour about a teaspoon of mixture into each tartlet. Bake for 15–20 minutes until puffed and the pastry is golden brown. Serve warm. These can be frozen and reheated.

Avocado, Prawn and Pink Ginger Rice Paper Rolls with Hoisin Dipping Sauce

Makes 24

For the rolls

24 rice paper wrappers
24 prawns, cooked and peeled
¼ cup Japanese pink pickled ginger
¼ cup coriander leaves
1 large avocado, firm but ripe, peeled and sliced

For the sauce

¼ cup sushi rice wine vinegar
2 tablespoons hoisin sauce
1 tablespoon sweet chilli sauce

To make the rolls, fill a large shallow dish with warm water. Dunk in a few rice paper wrappers and let them soften for about a minute. Remove and add a couple more to soak, while you prepare the first rolls.

Carefully lay the wrappers on the bench. Place a prawn, a slice of ginger, a few coriander leaves and an avocado slice on each wrapper and fold up, enclosing the filling in a neat little roll.

Wet a couple of paper towels in cold water and place on a small tray. Lay the rice paper rolls on this and cover with another couple of wet paper towels as you work. When they're all made, wrap the tray, wet paper towels included, in cling film until ready to serve.

To make the dipping sauce, whisk the ingredients together and serve in a small bowl beside the rolls.

Caperberries in a Crisp Cheese Pastry

These can be made well ahead of time, frozen and brought out to cook as required. You can also use the pastry to make cheese straws, pastry shells and quiche bases — it's really just a savoury version of my sweet pecan pie pastry.

Makes 36

100 g cold butter, cubed
100 g (large handful) grated tasty cheese
1 cup flour
½ teaspoon salt
36 caperberries, with stalks

Line a baking tray with non-stick baking paper.

Place butter, cheese, flour and salt in a food processor and run the machine until the pastry clumps around the blade. Gather the pastry in a ball and dunk in flour to coat.

Dry the caperberries with paper towel. Pinch off a piece of pastry, press out into a disc and wrap around a caperberry to enclose. Repeat until all the caperberries have been wrapped. Place on the prepared tray and put in the freezer for about 20 minutes until the pastry is quite hard.

Preheat the oven to 180°C. Bake the chilled caperberries for about 15–20 minutes, turning them so they evenly bake to a golden brown. Serve warm.

Cook School Tip

Caperberries are the grown-up version of little capers — much as a marrow is a grown-up courgette. Don't go overboard with the pastry on each one. Just make sure the caperberries are evenly covered without turning them into doughy mouthfuls.

See more Cook School Tips over the page

*Cook School Tips
for Crisp Cheese Pastry*

- You really need a food processor to make pastry for the caperberries recipe on page 20. The pastry clumps together as you run the machine. When the pastry has clumped into a ball, drop it into the flour bin to coat then shake off the excess flour. Wrap the ball of pastry in cling film and place in the fridge to harden and rest. (Pastry needs to rest to help the molecules in the gluten relax, which prevents it from shrinking and rising up when you cook it.)

- If you don't want to use the pastry right away, roll it into long salami-sized logs, wrap in cling film and freeze. You can then just chop off the amount you require to thaw. For easy cheese biscuits, thinly slice pieces off the roll and bake.

- Here are some other things to try wrapping with the pastry:

    - cubes of mozzarella cheese
    - halves of pickled onion with cubes of cheese
    - bits of blue cheese with fresh walnut halves
    - cocktail onions
    - baby gherkins
    - sundried tomatoes with cubes of feta
    - small chunks of salami with cubes of cheese.

- To freeze these tasty treats, lay them out in a single layer on a tray. Otherwise, store them free-flow in a sealed container or plastic bag. If cooking from frozen, just add a few extra minutes to the cooking time.

Blue Cheese and Spring Onion Dip

Serve this with carrot, celery and red capsicum sticks and corn chips.
A simple bowl of whole raw almonds is a nice easy and healthy nibble
to accompany this.

Makes approximately 2 cups

5 spring onions, chopped finely
125 g soft blue cheese (I use Blue Castello)
250 g lite sour cream
1 teaspoon Worcestershire sauce
salt and freshly ground black pepper
2 tablespoons chopped parsley

Place all ingredients in a food processor and pulse until blended, but still
retaining a little texture. Scrape into a serving bowl and chill. This can be made
a day ahead and stored, covered, in the fridge.

Parmesan Cheese Straws

Makes 40

1 cup finely grated Parmesan
1 teaspoon Mexican chilli powder or Cajun spice mix
1 teaspoon garlic salt
1 egg, beaten
2 sheets frozen flaky pastry, thawed

Preheat the oven to 200°C. Line two oven trays with non-stick baking paper or a silicone sheet.

Combine Parmesan, spice and garlic salt in a small bowl.

Paint the beaten egg over each sheet of pastry, then sprinkle with the Parmesan mixture. Using a rolling pin, gently press the mixture into the pastry. Turn the sheets over and repeat the painting and sprinkling. Fold each sheet in half and cut into strips, 20 from each sheet.

Twist the strips as you place them on the prepared trays. Bake for 20–25 minutes until puffed and golden. Cool on a wire rack. Store in an airtight container.

Pizza Pinwheels

Makes about 40

For the pinwheels	Optional extras
4 sheets frozen flaky pastry, thawed	canned crushed pineapple, drained
2 tablespoons spicy tomato sauce or	salami or sausage, sliced
BBQ sauce or tomato relish	mushrooms, finely sliced
2 cups grated tasty cheese	olives, sliced
12 rashers rindless streaky bacon	pesto
2 tablespoons chopped parsley	
1 handful basil leaves	
garlic salt	

Join two sheets of pastry together by brushing the edges with water and crimping with a fork. You need a good secure join. Do the same with the remaining two sheets of pastry. Brush the double sheets with tomato sauce then sprinkle with cheese and lay the bacon on top. Sprinkle with the herbs and garlic salt and any optional extras you may like.

Roll the short sides up tightly and secure the edges, by wetting them and using a fork to crimp the join so they won't unroll. Wrap in cling film and chill for at least an hour. (They can be frozen at this stage.)

Preheat the oven to 200°C. Line two oven trays with non-stick baking paper and spray well with baking spray. Slice the rolls into 5 mm slices and lay them flat on the trays, leaving room to expand and spread. (This can be done from frozen.) Bake for 10–15 minutes until puffed and golden, then turn over and bake another 5 minutes to evenly brown. Cool on a wire rack and serve warm.

Cook School Tip

You can make up any number of fillings for the basic pinwheel but always use ones with oil or natural fat, such as cheese or bacon, as this helps the pastry stay crisp and moist. You can reheat pinwheels, but I find it better to freeze them at the rolled-up stage then cut and cook as required.

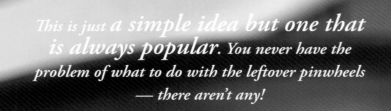

*This is just **a simple idea but one that is always popular**. You never have the problem of what to do with the leftover pinwheels — there aren't any!*

Preserved Figs

Fresh figs are one of the joys of gardening but you're often stuck with buckets full of them. What to do with them? Here is an answer.

Makes 8 x 500 ml jars

3 lemons, halved and thinly sliced
1 cup crystallised ginger, chopped finely (easy to do in a food processor)
2 cinnamon sticks
6 star anise pods
6 cardamom pods
½ cup malt vinegar
1.5 litres water
3 kg sugar
5 kg figs, picked over and wiped clean

Place all ingredients except the figs in a large saucepan and bring to the boil, stirring to dissolve the sugar. Add the figs and gently simmer with the lid on for 2 hours, until the figs are soft and glossy. Remove the whole spices.

Place figs in sterilised jars and fill to overflowing with the syrup. Cover and seal. Wash jars and store in a cool dark pantry for at least a month before serving. These will keep for 12–18 months.

Spicy Tiffin Eggs

This is a mini version of the ever-popular Scotch egg, with a good hint
of curry in the sausage meat. They are excellent to have with drinks or to
take on a picnic. For a picnic, remember to transport the eggs in a cool box
or chilly bin.

Makes 12

12 quail or small bantam eggs
700 g sausage meat
1 tablespoon mild curry paste
½ cup flour
2 eggs, beaten
1½ cups dried breadcrumbs
oil to deep fry

Hard boil the eggs, then cool in cold water. Crack and carefully peel off the
shells. Dry on paper towels.

Mix the sausage meat and curry paste together until well combined. Wet your
hands and press a portion of sausage meat mixture around each of the eggs. Dust
in the flour then dip in the beaten egg, then roll in the breadcrumbs to coat well.
Chill for at least an hour.

Deep fry in oil at 180°C for 6–7 minutes, cooking two or three at a time
and turning in the oil to evenly brown and ensure the sausage meat is cooked
through. Cool on paper towels and store in the fridge until ready to serve.

Easy

Easy to make, achievable, yet sophisticated.

Asparagus and Blue Cheese Bread Cases

Makes 24

olive oil spray
1 loaf sandwich-sliced brown or white bread
200 g soft blue cheese
1 cup grated tasty cheese
20 thin spears asparagus, sliced (can be canned)
3 eggs
1 cup cream
salt and freshly ground black pepper
¼ cup pine nuts (optional)

Preheat the oven to 200°C. Spray a 24-cup mini-muffin tin with olive oil.

Roll the slices of bread flat with a rolling pin and, using a 5–6 cm fluted cookie cutter, cut circles of bread and press into the prepared tins. Spray the cases with olive oil.

Divide the blue cheese, grated cheese and asparagus between the 24 cases. Whisk the eggs, cream, salt and pepper, and pine nuts if using, until well combined. Pour over the filling in each case.

Bake for 15–20 minutes until puffed and the cases are golden brown and crispy. Lift gently to check that the bases are cooked. Cool on a wire rack. Serve warm or at room temperature.

Pistachio Chicken Liver Pâté

Makes approximately 3 cups

50 g butter
2 packets (400 g) fresh chicken livers
1 large onion, finely chopped
4 cloves garlic, crushed (2 teaspoons)
¼ cup orange liqueur, brandy or fresh orange juice
200 g butter, cut into cubes
1 teaspoon ground cloves
½ teaspoon salt
1 teaspoon freshly ground black pepper
½ cup roughly chopped parsley
½ cup shelled pistachio nuts

Melt the first measure of butter in a large frypan and add the chicken livers, onion and garlic. Cook over medium heat until there is no pink left in the livers. Add the orange liqueur, brandy or juice and cook one more minute. Place the hot chicken liver mixture, including the liquid, in a food processor with the cubed butter, cloves, salt, pepper and parsley. Process until smooth. Taste and check the seasoning. (Sometimes a little extra salt is required.)

Divide the nuts in half. Add half to the food processor, then pulse the machine a few times to mix in the nuts but not completely chop them up. Spoon into small bowls and sprinkle the remaining pistachios over to garnish. Cover with cling film and store in the refrigerator, to set firmly. Serve with wholegrain toasts or crostini.

Bacon and Water Chestnuts

Water chestnuts will take on the flavour of whatever you cook them with.
They stay crunchy after cooking, with a texture a little like watermelon.
Simple and delish, this is one of my very favourite recipes. It is incredibly
popular at parties, particularly with teenagers. Just three ingredients and
away you go!

Makes approximately 60

2 x 225 g cans whole peeled water chestnuts
1 kg rindless streaky bacon
garlic salt

Preheat the oven to 200°C.

Drain the water chestnuts in a sieve. Cut the bacon in half crosswise and wrap
a half rasher around each water chestnut. Place in an oven dish or small roasting
tray and sprinkle with garlic salt. Roast for 15–20 minutes, turning once, until
bacon is crisp. Serve warm.

If made in advance, reheat for 5 minutes in a hot oven or reheat in a
microwave.

Cook School Tips

- *These can be made well ahead of time. Make, cook and freeze
a batch then relax, knowing you are ready for that impromptu
summer gathering.*
- *These are delicious with salad greens if serving a salad as a stand-
alone course, or are simply gorgeous as a side dish for the Christmas
turkey and ham.*
- *A water chestnut can, with both ends cut out, makes an ideal
mould for café-style individual servings of rice or couscous. It is also
the perfect size to cut pastry circles to line standard muffin tins.*

Arancini

The Italian name for these risotto balls means 'little oranges' and is inspired by
their rounded, golden look. Arancini are a traditional Sicilian dish.

Makes about 20 the size of golf balls

1 batch risotto, cooled to room temperature (use the recipe on page 178 or
you can use any leftover risotto)
1 cup flour
2 eggs, beaten
2 cups crisp, dry breadcrumbs
oil to deep fry

With wet hands, roll risotto into golf ball-sized balls, squeezing firmly into
shape. Roll balls in flour then dip in the egg and roll in breadcrumbs. Deep fry
in oil at 190°C for 2–3 minutes, cooking three to four at a time and turning in
the oil to evenly brown. Drain on a paper towel and serve warm.

Cook School Tip

*Here's a chance to use any leftovers lurking about in your fridge.
Various things can be buried in the centre of the risotto balls.
Try cubes of cheese and/or ham, sundried tomatoes and pickles.
Try adding chopped fresh herbs to the risotto.*

Ploughman's Pasties

*Pasties can be eaten warm or cold. I usually cook these on the morning
of a picnic and wrap them in a clean tea towel so they're still
just warm at lunchtime.*

Makes 6

3 sheets frozen flaky pastry, thawed
2 large handfuls grated tasty cheese
3 medium potatoes, boiled, then cooled and cut into small cubes
2 cups chopped pickled onions
½ cup ploughman's relish or pickle
2 tablespoons chopped parsley
1 egg, separated
2 teaspoons sesame seeds

Preheat the oven to 180°C.

Cut two small saucer shapes out of each sheet of pastry — you may need to
roll the pastry out a little to get two from each sheet. In a bowl, mix the grated
cheese, potato cubes, pickled onions, ploughman's relish, parsley and egg white.
Divide the mixture evenly, spooning into the centre of each of the six pastry
circles.

Brush the edges of the pastry with water and bring them up around the filling,
pinching together to envelop it completely in a traditional pasty shape. Mix the
egg yolk with 1 teaspoon of water and brush over the pasties to glaze. Sprinkle
with sesame seeds and chill in the fridge for 10–15 minutes.

Bake for 20–25 minutes until puffed and golden brown. Cool on a wire rack.

Pumpkin and Chive Mini Frittatas

Makes 24

2 cups peeled and grated pumpkin
1 cup grated tasty cheese
3 tablespoons chopped chives
6 eggs, beaten
¼ cup milk
salt and freshly ground black pepper
3 tablespoons pumpkin seeds (optional)

Preheat the oven to 180°C. Spray a 24-cup mini-muffin tin with baking spray, or use a silicone muffin tray.

Mix all ingredients together except the pumpkin seeds. Spoon into the prepared muffin tin and sprinkle with the pumpkin seeds, if using. Bake for 25 minutes until set and golden brown. Cool on a wire rack, still in the tin. When cool enough to handle, carefully turn out of the tin and serve warm.

Bangkok-style Fish Cakes with Sesame Dipping Sauce

Serves 4

For the fish cakes
800 g firm white fish fillets
1–2 cloves garlic, crushed (½ teaspoon)
1 teaspoon deseeded and chopped fresh chilli
2 tablespoons chopped coriander leaves
freshly ground black pepper
1 teaspoon Asian fish sauce
1 teaspoon grated fresh ginger
oil to shallow fry

For the dipping sauce
4 tablespoons sweet chilli sauce
grated rind and juice of 2 limes
1 teaspoon sesame oil
1 tablespoon lite soy sauce

To make the fish cakes, place all ingredients except the oil in a food processor and run the machine until a coarse paste is formed. Shape heaped teaspoons of the mixture into little cakes.

Heat a little oil in a large non-stick frypan and cook the fish cakes in batches, turning after 2 minutes and cooking for another 2 minutes until golden brown on both sides. Drain on paper towels and keep warm as you cook the remainder of the mixture.

To make the dipping sauce, place all the ingredients in a screw-top jar and shake together until well blended.

Serve warm fish cakes with dipping sauce.

Melting Cheese and Chive Pastries

These can be made in advance, but are nicest served just warm.

Makes 24

1 cup grated tasty cheese
1 cup flour
½ teaspoon garlic salt
100 g cold butter, cut into cubes
2 tablespoons snipped chives

Place grated cheese, flour, garlic salt and butter in a food processor and run the machine until a clump of pastry forms around the blade. Add the chives and process for just a few seconds to incorporate them into the dough.

Form the pastry into a sausage-shaped log and wrap in cling film. Freeze for 30 minutes until quite cold and solid.

Preheat the oven to 180°C. Spray a baking tray with baking spray. Slice the log into small discs like small coins. Place on the prepared tray and chill in the freezer for 10 more minutes.

Bake pastries for 10–12 minutes until pale golden brown. Cool on a wire rack. Store in an airtight container.

SEAGARS

Easy

Easy entertaining may seem like a contradiction in terms, but it's what I'm all about.

Snap, Crackle and Popcorn Chicken

Colonel You-know-who and Mr Rice Bubble might get a bit 'thingie' about
the naming of this recipe but it is the best way to describe this delicious nibbly
chicken that's perfect for snacks with drinks.

Serves 4–6

½ cup arrowroot
½ cup cornflour
2 teaspoons Cajun spice mix
4 boneless and skinless chicken breasts, cut into 1 cm cubes
2 eggs, beaten well
oil to deep fry

Mix the arrowroot, cornflour and Cajun spice together. Toss the chicken in the
egg, mixing well to evenly coat. Toss the chicken pieces in the flour and spice
mixture and shake off any excess.

Deep fry in oil at 190°C in batches, for 2–3 minutes for each batch. Drain on
paper towels. Serve immediately.

Bacon, Spinach and Haloumi Rolls

Haloumi is a semi-firm cheese made from sheep's milk that is sold
in small blocks, usually in a little brine. It is readily available in
delicatessens and most supermarkets.

Makes 20

20 large spinach (or silverbeet) leaves
180 g Haloumi
10 rashers rindless streaky bacon
garlic salt

Preheat the oven to 200°C.

Wash the spinach leaves, discard the stalks and microwave on high for 1–1½
minutes to wilt. Drain on paper towels. Cut the cheese into 20 pieces and wrap
each piece in a wilted spinach leaf. Cut bacon rashers in half and wrap each half
around a spinach parcel, securing with a toothpick.

Line a 20 cm x 30 cm slice tin with non-stick baking paper. Place the parcels
in the prepared tin and sprinkle with garlic salt. Bake for 10–15 minutes until
the bacon is crisp. You may need to turn them over and cook for a few minutes
longer. Remove the toothpicks and serve warm, but not directly from the oven
as the filling can be very hot and gooey.

Many people are having great success growing fabulous olives, but some have no idea what to do with them once they've got a bucketful. Here's the answer. I like olives to be a bit salty and like to have them in a selection of flavours to match with different dishes, cheeses, etc.

1 Collect ripe (black) olives or green olives that are turning browny-black.

2 Pick over the olives, discarding any soft or damaged fruit.

3 Make a small cut or slit in each olive and place immediately in cold water. Keep the olives covered with water for the next 10 days, draining and replacing the water each day. This is necessary to leach out the bitterness that olives have in their raw state.

4 Make a brine using 1 cup uniodised salt to 10 cups water. Dissolve the salt and bring to the boil, then cool. Place the olives in sterilised jars. (I give mine a wash and get them straight out of the dishwasher.) Cover with the brine and top each jar with 1 cm olive oil. (The oil forms a protective barrier over the olives and stops air getting to them.) Screw on the lids.

5 Store for a year in a cool pantry, then drain off the brine and taste the olives. If they are bit salty, fill the jars with water and leave for 24 hours. Repeat this process until they taste just as you like them.

6 When the olives are to your liking, drain off the water and fill the jars with olive oil, adding herbs and garlic, lemon or orange zest, chillies or cloves to taste.

#

There is nothing nicer to team with cheese than these simple biscuits.
They are delicious served with quince paste and blue cheese.

Makes about 20 biscuits

———

2 tablespoons flaxseeds (also known as linseed)
¾ cup wholemeal flour
½ cup self-raising flour
2 tablespoons brown sugar
1 teaspoon salt
100 g butter, cut into small cubes
1 cup rolled oats
1 egg
1–2 teaspoons boiling water
1 handful flaxseeds

Preheat the oven to 180°C. Spread two oven trays with non-stick baking paper or use a silicone mat.

Place flaxseeds, flours, brown sugar, salt and butter in a food processor and run the machine until the mixture resembles coarse breadcrumbs. Add the rolled oats and run the machine to just mix them in. (You don't want to over-process and chop the oats too much, as this will affect the texture.)

Add the egg and a little boiling water, pulsing the machine until the dough clumps in a ball. Knead briefly and shape into a flattened round. Roll on a lightly floured board or, better still, a silicone sheet that does not require any flour. Roll out to 4–5 mm thick. Use a 7 cm round cookie cutter to cut out circles and place on prepared trays. Sprinkle flaxseeds on top. The biscuits don't spread out much so they can be placed quite close together.

Bake for 25–30 minutes until crisp and dry looking. Cool on a wire rack and store in an airtight container.

Chickpea Parmesan Pennies with Minted Yoghurt Sauce

These are great to serve with drinks, as a vegetarian main or as a side dish
to accompany barbecued chicken.

Serves 4–6

For the pennies

2 x 400 g cans chickpeas, drained and rinsed
2–3 cloves garlic, crushed (1 teaspoon)
1 teaspoon ground cumin
1 small red onion, peeled and finely chopped
3 tablespoons chopped coriander leaves
¾ cup finely grated Parmesan
flour for handling
oil to fry

For the sauce

250 g thick natural yoghurt
½ cup prepared mint jelly
1–2 cloves garlic, crushed (½ teaspoon)
2 tablespoons chopped parsley

To make the pennies, place chickpeas, garlic, cumin, onion, coriander and
Parmesan in a food processor and run the machine to form a smooth paste.

With floured hands, shape into 20 small flat circles, like pennies. Heat oil in
a large non-stick frypan and cook pennies in batches for a couple of minutes on
each side until browned. Keep warm as you cook the remainder of the mixture.

To make the sauce, mix all ingredients together and store, covered, in the
fridge.

Serve warm pennies with yoghurt sauce at room temperature.

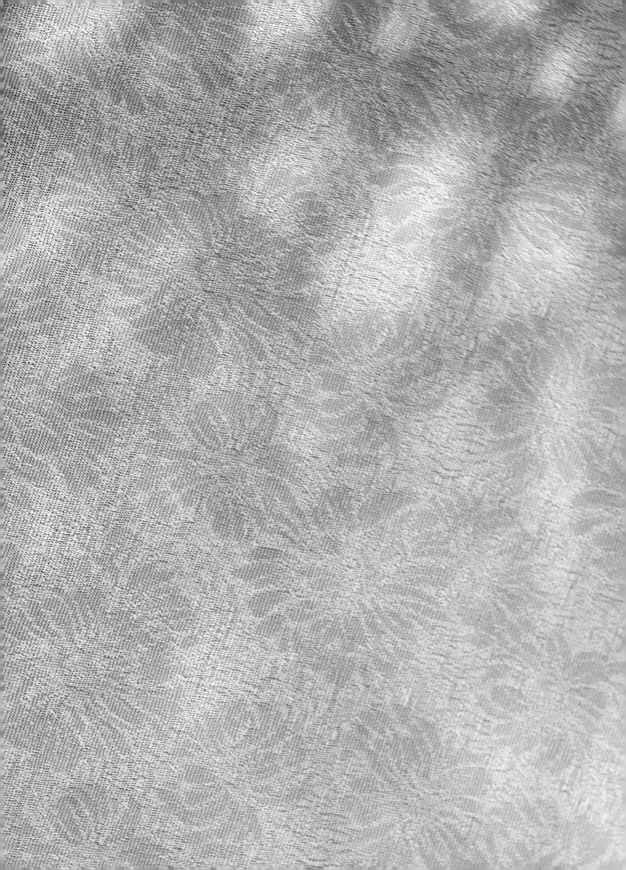

2. Soups & Breads

I don't think real friends go home from a dinner party at your house and say, 'I don't think she made her own mayonnaise.' Get over the feeling that entertaining is a test. No one is going to be there with a clipboard giving you marks out of one hundred.

Asian Noodle Soup

Serves 4

For the soup

1 litre chicken stock

1 tablespoon lite soy sauce

1 teaspoon grated fresh ginger

2 tablespoons sweet chilli sauce

1 packet instant or Singapore-style noodles

2 cups shrimps or prawns, peeled and cooked

1 teaspoon sesame oil

1 handful mung bean sprouts or snowpea shoots

1 small bunch coriander leaves, chopped

1 small red chilli, deseeded and sliced

Optional extras

coconut cream

beans, sliced

asparagus, sliced

spring onions, sliced

mushrooms, sliced

Bring the chicken stock, soy sauce, ginger and sweet chilli sauce to the boil. Add the noodles and shrimps or prawns. Simmer for 3–4 minutes to soften the noodles. Add the remaining ingredients, including any optional extras you desire, and serve in small Asian noodle bowls.

Spinach, Lemon and Rice Soup

I often make this Greek-style soup with brown rice or lentils, which take
a little longer to cook — both are good substitutes for white rice.
Serve it piping hot with lots of wholemeal toast or, better still,
cheese melted and bubbling on toast. Yum!

Serves 4–6

2 tablespoons olive oil
2 onions, roughly chopped
2–3 cloves garlic, crushed (1 teaspoon)
2 large potatoes, peeled and cut into pea-sized dice
6 cups good chicken stock
1 kg spinach or young tender silverbeet leaves, washed and shredded
½ cup rice
grated rind and juice of 2 lemons
salt and freshly ground black pepper

Heat oil in a large saucepan and cook onions until well softened. Add garlic,
potato, chicken stock, spinach, rice and lemon rind and juice. Simmer for 30
minutes, checking that there is enough liquid as the rice absorbs it. Add water if
required. Season as desired.

Indian Spiced Lentil Soup

This is great with naan or poppadams for an easy Sunday-night tea.

Serves 4–6

2 tablespoons oil (rice bran or canola)
2 onions, chopped finely
2–3 cloves garlic, crushed (1 teaspoon)
1½ litres good chicken or vegetable stock
1 cup lentils (red split lentils or green lentils)
2 handfuls spinach leaves, washed and finely sliced
1 tablespoon garam masala
2 teaspoons mild curry paste
1 x 400 ml can coconut cream
salt and freshly ground black pepper
½ cup chopped parsley

Heat oil in a large saucepan and cook the onions until well softened. Add the garlic, stock, lentils, spinach, garam masala and curry paste. Bring to the boil then reduce heat and simmer for 15 minutes until the lentils are well cooked.

In a blender, purée three-quarters of the soup. Return to the saucepan and mix with the coconut cream. Season as desired and add the chopped parsley just before serving.

Creamy Kumara and Chilli Soup

Serves 6

For the soup

2 tablespoons olive oil

50 g butter

2 large onions, peeled and chopped

2–3 cloves garlic, crushed (1 teaspoon)

6 kumara, peeled and chopped into even-sized pieces

5 small chillies, finely chopped

½ cup chopped coriander leaves

2 litres well-flavoured beef, chicken or vegetable stock

salt and freshly ground black pepper

cream, milk or extra stock to achieve desired consistency (if required)

For the garnish

sour cream

shaved Parmesan

chopped coriander leaves

sliced red chillies

Heat the oil and butter in a large saucepan. Add the chopped onion and garlic and fry for 2–3 minutes to soften. Add the kumara cubes, chilli, coriander and stock. Simmer until the kumara is tender. Process or blend until smooth and season as desired. Thin the soup with cream, milk or extra stock if desired.

Garnish by swirling in a dollop of sour cream and top with Parmesan, coriander and chillies.

Courgette and Bacon Soup

This is the perfect answer to winter soup cravings. It is quick to make and always hits the spot.

Serves 4

2 tablespoons olive oil
6 rashers rindless bacon, chopped
2 medium onions, peeled and chopped
2–3 cloves garlic, crushed (1 teaspoon)
2 litres chicken stock
1 teaspoon Worcestershire sauce
3–4 mashing potatoes (Agria or Desiree), peeled and chopped
6 medium courgettes, sliced or chopped
½ cup chopped parsley
½ cup sour cream or crème fraîche
½ cup finely grated Parmesan
salt and finely ground black pepper

Heat oil in a saucepan and fry bacon until browned. Remove bacon and fry the onions and garlic until softened (3–4 minutes). Add the stock, Worcestershire sauce, potatoes, courgettes and parsley. Bring to the boil then turn down the heat and simmer for about 10 minutes, until the potato is cooked.

In a blender, purée the soup with the sour cream and Parmesan until smooth and season as desired. Stir through the bacon and serve immediately with warm soft bread rolls or cheesy toasts.

Smoked Salmon and Prawn Chowder

I love seafood chowders and know a lot of you do, too. This recipe is always popular on our menu and we're constantly asked for it by visitors to the café. Chowder develops a delicious smokiness over time so I recommend you make it a day or two before you intend to serve it.

Serves 6

For the chowder
50 g butter
2 leeks, washed and finely sliced
4 tablespoons flour
4 medium potatoes, peeled and cut into even-sized cubes
1 litre milk
1 litre good fish, chicken or vegetable stock
1 x 310 g can smoked fish fillets
1 cup smoked salmon offcuts or hot-smoked salmon flakes
2 cups prawns, peeled and cooked
salt and freshly ground black pepper

Optional extras
1 cup cream
½ cup chopped parsley
2 tablespoons chopped dill

Heat butter in a large saucepan. Add the sliced leeks and cook for 3–4 minutes until softened. Add the flour and cook for a minute before adding the potatoes, milk and stock. Stir while bringing to the boil, then turn down and simmer for 10–15 minutes until the potato is tender. Add the contents of the can of fish (including the liquid), smoked salmon and prawns. Season as desired.

Simmer for another 10–15 minutes and serve straight away or cool and store in the fridge for later. Add the cream, parsley and dill just before serving, if using.

Beef and Barley Soup

This makes a big potful and, with a bit of crusty or garlic bread, is all you need for a heart-warming lunch.

Serves 6–8

10 g dried porcini mushrooms
2 tablespoons extra-virgin olive oil
1 kg chuck or blade steak, cut into cubes
2 large onions, chopped
4–5 cloves garlic, crushed (2 teaspoons)
3 stalks celery, sliced
2 carrots, peeled and diced
250 g sliced button mushrooms (3 cups)
3 cups water
4 cups good-flavoured beef stock
2 cups barley
½ cup chopped parsley
salt and freshly ground black pepper

Place porcini in a small bowl and cover with boiling water. Soak for 20 minutes. Drain, but reserve the liquid. Chop the porcini and set aside.

Heat oil in a large saucepan and fry the steak cubes until browned. Remove and then add the onion, garlic, celery, carrots and mushrooms to the pan. Cook these until browned. Return the beef to the saucepan and add the water, reserved porcini liquid, stock, barley and porcini.

Simmer for an hour, stirring every now and then. Add more water if the soup becomes too thick. Stir to break up the meat. Add chopped parsley just before serving and season as desired.

Flatbread on the Barbecue

A silicone barbecue sheet over the hot plate makes a lovely clean non-stick
surface to cook these on. It is also useful for pancakes and fried eggs
on the barbecue.

Makes 10

1½ teaspoons active dried yeast
½ teaspoon honey or sugar
1¼ cups warm water
3 cups high-grade flour
2 teaspoons salt
4 tablespoons olive oil
1 handful black sesame seeds (optional)

Place the yeast, honey or sugar and water in a small bowl, whisking to mix well.
Let it stand until the mixture is frothy (about 10 minutes). Add the flour, salt
and olive oil and knead until the dough is smooth and elastic. (This can be done
in an electric mixer fitted with a dough hook.) Oil a bowl and place the dough
in it. Cover the bowl with cling film and stand the bowl in a warm place for
about 1½ hours until the dough has doubled in size.

Punch the dough down and divide into 12 small balls. Roll these into flatbread
discs. Sprinkle with black sesame seeds if using.

Preheat the barbecue plate. When hot, place as many flatbreads as you can fit
on the plate and cook for 2–3 minutes before turning over and cooking for a
further 2–3 minutes. Keep warm as you cook the remainder of the mixture.

Beer Bread

This is a wonderful, quick bread that has the texture, taste and, best of all, the smell of a lovely fresh-from-the-oven farmhouse loaf. This recipe doesn't work with low-alcohol beer or stout.

Makes 1 large or 2 small loaves

3 cups flour
3 teaspoons baking powder
1 teaspoon salt
1 x 330 ml can or bottle beer, made up to
400 ml with water (just rinse out the can)
1 handful grated cheese (½ cup)

Preheat the oven to 200°C. Grease a 20 cm x 10 cm loaf tin or two 8 cm x 15 cm loaf tins. Alternatively, use non-stick loaf tins.

Mix the flour, baking powder, salt and beer in a large bowl until well combined. Tip into the prepared tin or tins and sprinkle grated cheese on top.

Bake the large loaf for 50–60 minutes or the small loaves for 25–30 minutes, until golden brown. Tip out and cool on a wire rack before slicing. This bread keeps well and also makes excellent toast.

Cook School Tip

For a quick and easy lunch for unexpected guests, mix a spoonful of curry paste into a can of pumpkin soup. Then whip up a batch of beer bread and bake it in an 8-cup mini-loaf tin for 10–15 minutes. Sprinkle some chopped fresh coriander leaves on top of the soup when serving. Hey presto — a tasty lunch in next to no time!

See Beer Bread Inspirations over the page

Beer Bread Inspirations

The basic beer bread recipe is incredibly versatile. Once you have made a
batch, you might like to try some of the following ideas:

- Make foccacia by spraying a 20 cm x 30 cm slice tin with baking spray.
  Spread the beer dough into the prepared tin and sprinkle with 1 tablespoon
  of rock salt or sea salt flakes and 1 tablespoon fresh rosemary leaves. Spray the
  top with olive oil. Bake for 20–25 minutes until golden brown. Cool on a
  wire rack before slicing.

- Make hot cross buns by adding ½ cup caster sugar, ½ cup sultanas,
  ½ cup currants, 2 tablespoons mixed peel and 1 teaspoon mixed spice to
  the basic recipe.

  Spray a regular-sized 12-cup muffin tin with baking spray. Divide the
  dough into 12 equal portions and place one in each muffin cup.

  Mix 2 tablespoons of water and 2 tablespoons of flour in a small ziplock
  bag, cut off the corner and pipe crosses on top of each bun. Bake for 15–20
  minutes until golden brown. Brush tops with golden syrup or honey as they
  come out of the oven. Cool on a wire rack before serving warm with butter.

- Place half the beer dough into the tin, add a layer of blue cheese and walnuts
  or olives and sundried tomatoes, and cover with the remaining dough.

- For a crowd, make two to three batches and cook the bread in a roasting dish
  or large cake tin.

- Use half wholemeal and half white flour.

- Add nuts, seeds and chopped garlic to the basic dough.

- Different beers add different flavours.

- Press the dough flat to use as a pizza base. Just add your favourite toppings
  and you're away! Make sure your pizza tray has an edge to contain the dough.

Slow

Slow down, simplify,
be generous.

Spicy Breadsticks

These Italian-style crispy breadsticks are known in Italy as grissini. They can be served on their own or as a part of a large nibbly platter.

Makes 40

2 teaspoons active dried yeast
1 teaspoon honey
1 cup warm water
2½ cups high-grade flour
1 teaspoon salt
2 teaspoons caraway seeds

1 tablespoon ground cumin
1 tablespoon ground coriander
2 tablespoons olive oil
1 egg, beaten
3 tablespoons flaky salt

Place yeast, honey and warm water in a large bowl or use an electric mixer fitted with a dough hook. Mix, then rest for 15 minutes until the yeast is good and frothy.

Add the flour, salt, spices and olive oil and mix to form a soft pliable dough. Knead for a few minutes until non-sticky and elastic. Place the dough in an oiled mixing bowl, cover with cling film and set aside until the dough has doubled in size.

Line two oven trays with non-stick baking paper and spray with oil. Punch down the dough and knead for 3 minutes then roll into long, ropey sausage shapes, about 20 cm long. Lay these on prepared trays, cover with cling film and leave for 30 minutes to rise.

Preheat the oven to 200°C. Brush bread sticks with beaten egg and generously sprinkle with flaky salt. Bake for 20–25 minutes until golden brown. Cool on a wire rack.

Cook School Tip

The spicy breadstick dough can be frozen after you have punched it down or when you have rolled it into the long rope shapes. Freeze the ropes on the tray then carefully remove and store frozen in ziplock bags. Defrost on prepared trays before baking.

Spiced Pumpkin Bread

This is dead easy, and perfect for a last-minute brunch or late-lunch treat.

Makes 2 loaves

1 cup oil
2 cups sugar
3 eggs
2 cups grated pumpkin
½ teaspoon salt
2 teaspoons mixed spice
1 teaspoon ground cloves
3 cups high-grade flour
3 teaspoons baking powder
1 cup chopped walnuts or pecans

Preheat the oven to 180°C. Spray two 20 cm x 10 cm loaf tins with baking spray. Beat the oil, sugar and eggs together until creamy. Mix in the other ingredients and spoon into the prepared tins. Bake for 1 hour until golden brown. Cool on a wire rack.

Artichoke Foccacia Bread

This foccacia freezes very well. It also keeps well for a couple of days stored in a bread bin.

2 teaspoons active dried yeast
1 teaspoon honey
350 ml warm water (warm bath temperature)
3½ cups high-grade flour
1 teaspoon salt, plus extra to sprinkle
3 tablespoons olive oil
1 x 450 g jar artichoke hearts in oil, drained and chopped
freshly ground black pepper
1 sprig fresh rosemary or 2 tablespoons rosemary leaves
1 tablespoon coarsely ground rock salt

Place the yeast, honey and warm water in a large bowl, preferably the bowl of an electric mixer fitted with a dough hook. Run the machine for a few seconds to combine, then leave for 10 minutes until the yeast is starting to get frothy. Add the flour, salt and olive oil and mix until the dough has balled up and become smooth and elastic. If doing by hand, knead for 6–7 minutes until the dough is shiny and quite soft. Use extra flour on your hands and the bench to produce a smooth dough.

Spray or oil a bowl, place the dough in it and cover with cling film. Put the bowl in a warm place for at least an hour until the dough has doubled in size. Punch the dough down and work it into a large round shape. Cover one half of the round with the chopped artichokes and sprinkle with salt and freshly ground black pepper. Fold over the other half of the dough to enclose the artichokes. Press the edges down to seal. Brush the surface of the dough generously with some of the oil from the artichoke jar, and sprinkle with rosemary leaves and rock salt. Cover loosely with cling film and allow to rise for a further 30 minutes.

Preheat the oven to 200°C. Remove the cling film and place on an oven tray. Bake the dough for 25–30 minutes until golden brown and risen. Turn down the temperature to 170°C and bake for a further 15 minutes. Cool on a wire rack. Cut with a bread knife into long, thin slices.

Lavash Bread

These crisp Armenian crackers make a delicious alternative to
chippies or can be served with cheese.

Makes 50

½ cup wholemeal flour
3 cups flour
2 teaspoons salt
2 tablespoons poppy seeds
2 tablespoons sesame seeds
1 egg
1 cup milk
60 g butter, melted

Spray two oven trays with baking spray.

Mix all the ingredients together to form a soft, elastic dough. Knead for a few
minutes until more elastic. Divide into 8–10 pieces. Roll out each of these then
run them through a pasta machine on one of the finest settings to make long,
thin sheets. Cut into standard crispbread sizes and place on the oven trays. Allow
to dry for about an hour.

Preheat the oven to 180°C. Bake 10–12 minutes until golden, crispy and dry.
Cool on a wire rack and store in an airtight container.

3. Filling the Tins

I'm a big believer in the value of
getting around the table as a family
or with good friends and taking
time to enjoy each other's company.
It's about being thankful and happy
together and counting your blessings.
And it might be as simple as a cup of
tea with some nice baking.

Rum and Raisin Apple Cake

½ cup rum (white or dark)

2 cups sugar

3 eggs

¾ cup oil

2 teaspoons vanilla essence

2½ cups flour

2 teaspoons baking powder

2 teaspoons ground cinnamon

1 teaspoon salt

4 large apples (Granny Smith or Braeburn),
peeled, cored and cut into 1 cm dice

1 cup chopped walnuts

1 cup raisins

Preheat the oven to 180°C. Spray a 24 cm kugelhopf pan or a 23–25 cm spring-form tin with baking spray.

Simmer the rum in a small saucepan until it has reduced by half. Beat the sugar and eggs together and add the oil, vanilla and reduced rum. Mix in the dry ingredients, apple, walnuts and raisins. Scrape into the prepared tin and bake for approximately 40 minutes, until a skewer comes out clean and the cake has pulled away from the sides of the tin.

Cool in the tin for 5 minutes then carefully turn out onto a wire rack and cool further. Serve with softly whipped cream or yoghurt and, if desired, a dusting of icing sugar.

White Chocolate Caramel Oat Cake

**Keep this delicious cake chilled in the fridge ready to serve with thick yoghurt,
whipped cream or ice cream — or all three!**

For the caramel
1 x 400 g can sweetened condensed milk
2 tablespoons golden syrup
150 g butter

For the cake
1½ cups wholemeal flour
¾ cup flour
2 teaspoons baking powder
½ teaspoon baking soda
1½ cups rolled oats
1½ cups brown sugar, firmly packed
¾ cup dessicated coconut
2 eggs
250 g butter, melted
1 tablespoon vanilla essence
1 cup white chocolate buttons

To make the caramel, place all the ingredients in a small saucepan and stir over
a medium heat until well combined and smooth. Allow to cool.

Preheat the oven to 180°C. Spray a 25–26 cm spring-form tin with baking
spray and line the base with non-stick baking paper.

To make the cake, place all the dry ingredients except the chocolate buttons
in a large bowl and mix well. Beat the eggs, melted butter and vanilla together
then mix into the dry ingredients. Press three-quarters of this mixture into the
prepared tin. Pour over the caramel, then crumble the remaining cake mixture
on top.

Bake for 45 minutes, until golden brown. Cool completely in the tin. When
cold, melt the white chocolate buttons in the microwave and drizzle over the top
of the cake.

Very Easy Fruitcake

This is a quick, easy cake with hardly any ingredients, but it's always well
received and it keeps in a tin really well — good to have in the pantry.
It's also great without the frosting.

For the cake
1 kg mixed dried fruit
2 teaspoons mixed spice
2 cups pure orange juice (from a carton is fine)
2 cups self-raising flour

For the frosting
125 g butter
2 tablespoons brandy
3 cups icing sugar (approximately)

Preheat the oven to 160°C. Spray a 23 cm cake tin with baking spray.

To make the cake, mix all the ingredients in a large bowl and transfer to the
prepared tin. Bake for 1 hour then turn the oven down to 150°C and bake for a
further 45–60 minutes, until a skewer inserted into the centre comes out clean
and the cake is firm and pulling away from the sides of the tin. Cool in the tin
for an hour before turning out and cooling further on a wire rack.

To make the frosting, beat the butter and brandy together with 2 cups of
icing sugar, then add as much of the third cup as is needed to produce a fluffy
frosting. Ice the top and sides of the cooled cake then allow the icing to set for
3–4 hours before serving. But watch out for sneaky pinchers of the frosting — it
is very more-ish.

Giant Prize-winning Fabbo Sponge Cake

1 cup sugar
2 tablespoons water
4 eggs, separated
few drops of vanilla essence
1½ cups wheaten cornflour
1 teaspoon baking powder
½ teaspoon salt
lightly whipped cream to serve
fresh or preserved fruit or berries to serve
icing sugar to dust

Preheat the oven to 180°C. Spray two shallow 21 cm sponge tins with baking spray and line the bases with non-stick baking paper.

Place sugar and water in a small saucepan and bring to the boil, or microwave. Using an electric mixer fitted with a whisk attachment, beat the egg whites until stiff. With the mixer running, slowly dribble in the hot sugar and water solution. Beat really hard. Add the egg yolks and vanilla then carefully fold in the sifted dry ingredients. Be very gentle with the folding process. Carefully pour into the prepared tins and bake for 18–20 minutes. As soon as you remove the sponges from the oven, drop the tins from knee height square on the floor — no kidding! This is an odd but tried-and-true sponge-making trick that somehow 'shocks' the cake and stops it deflating. Take out of the tin immediately and cool on a wire rack.

When cool, sandwich the two sponges together with cream and fresh or preserved fruit. Dust the top with icing sugar and cut with a serrated knife.

Cook School Tip

This recipe needs the gluten in the cornflour to make it all stick together. It can not be made with gluten-free cornflour.

Always a winner at A & P shows, this cake is *impressive for afternoon tea*, to show off for the vicar *or to serve as dessert* with lashings of whipped cream or ice cream and fruit.

Those famous *heart-warming words:* 'I'll put the kettle on for a nice cuppa and we'll deal with this together.'

Kumara and Orange Cake with Citrus Cream Cheese Frosting

For the cake
3½ cups flour
3 teaspoons baking powder
2 teaspoons baking soda
3 teaspoons ground cinnamon
3½ cups brown sugar
1½ cups sultanas
1½ cups walnuts
5 cups grated golden kumara (2 large kumara)
5 eggs
350 ml oil
2 tablespoons fresh orange juice
grated rind of 3 oranges

For the frosting
400 g regular cream cheese
100 g butter, softened to room temperatures
4 cups icing sugar (approximately)
grated rind of 2 oranges
chopped nuts (optional)

Preheat the oven to 180°C. Spray a large, deep 28–30 cm spring-form cake tin with baking spray and line the base with non-stick baking paper.

To make the cake, place all the dry ingredients with the sultanas and walnuts in a large bowl. Mix in the grated kumara. In a separate bowl, beat the eggs, oil, orange juice and rind together then mix into the dry ingredients. Pour into the prepared tin and bake for 45 minutes, then turn the oven down to 160°C and bake for a further 30–35 minutes until a skewer inserted into the centre comes out clean and the cake is firm and pulling away from the sides of the tin. Turn out onto a wire rack to cool.

To make the frosting, beat all the ingredients except the nuts and grated rind together until smooth and a good spreading consistency. Frost the cooled cake and sprinkle rind on top and chopped nuts on the sides if desired.

This is like a carrot cake, but has a *unique kumara flavour* — perfect for showing off a few local flavours to overseas visitors.

*Lots of experimenting with mud cake recipes has produced this **chocolate-lovers' dream cake**. It is the most popular dessert in our café. The rich mousse filling is so good for you — your soul, that is! You'll need to allow 2 days to produce this cake but serve it with softly whipped cream or ice cream and berries or fruit and wait for the accolades to pour in!* **You won't be disappointed.**

Seagars Chocolate Mud Cake

For the cake	For the filling
1¾ cups flour	2 cups cream
1¾ cups sugar	450 g dark chocolate, chopped
2 teaspoons baking soda	6 egg yolks
¾ cup baking cocoa	½ cup caster sugar
1 teaspoon salt	
1½ cups milk	For the ganache
100 g butter, melted	180 ml milk
2 eggs	225 ml cream
1 teaspoon vanilla	750 g chopped dark chocolate

Preheat the oven to 180°C. Spray a deep 23–25 cm spring-form cake tin with baking spray and line the base with non-stick baking paper.

To make the cake, place all the ingredients in the bowl of an electric mixer and beat until smoothly combined. Pour into the prepared tin and bake for 50–55 minutes until firm in the centre, and the cake is pulling away from the sides of the tin. Cool in the tin on a wire rack until completely cold.

To make the filling, place cream and chocolate in a medium-sized saucepan and heat gently, stirring, until smoothly combined. Set aside to cool.

Place egg yolks and caster sugar in a bowl over a saucepan of warm water. Beat with a hand-held electric mixer on high for 5–6 minutes until the mixture is pale and creamy. Mix in the chocolate and cream and beat for an additional 5–6 minutes. Chill the mixture for at least 30 minutes.

To assemble the cake, cut the cake in half horizontally. Line the original cake tin with cling film, allowing a good overhang. Place half of the cake in the lined tin, then pour in the filling and top with the other half of the cake. Fold the cling film over to cover the cake, and refrigerate for 8–10 hours or until the next day.

Before serving, make the ganache by placing the ingredients in a medium-sized saucepan and stirring over gentle heat. Stir until it comes to the boil and make sure the chocolate is melted and the mixture smooth. Cool to room temperature.

Remove the cake from the plastic-lined tin and place on a wire rack over a tray to catch the overflow. Gently drizzle the ganache over the cake, covering the top and sides. The overflow can be scraped up and used again to get a thick, even glaze over the entire cake. Cover loosely with cling film and keep in the fridge to set the ganache. Keep chilled until ready to serve.

Raspberry Cheesecake-Swirl Brownies

Serve these as a dessert with cream and raspberry sauce or store in an airtight container to serve with coffee.

Makes 24

For the brownie
4 eggs
2 cups caster sugar
150 g butter
375 g dark chocolate melts
1 cup flour
½ teaspoon baking powder
¾ cup cocoa
1 teaspoon vanilla esssence
1 cup or large handful fresh or frozen
    raspberries (do not thaw)

For the cheesecake
250 g tub regular cream cheese
1 egg
½ cup icing sugar
3 tablespoons flour

Preheat the oven to 170°C. Spray a 23 cm x 23 cm brownie tin with baking spray and line with tinfoil or non-stick baking paper.

To make the brownie, beat the eggs and caster sugar in a large mixing bowl until pale and creamy. In a microwave, or over a pot of simmering water, melt the butter and chocolate, stirring until smooth. Add the egg and sugar mixture, then mix in the flour, baking powder, cocoa and vanilla.

In a separate bowl, beat all the cheesecake ingredients together until smooth.

Spoon the chocolate and cheesecake mixtures alternately into the prepared tin and dot the raspberries on top. Gently, with a knife, swirl the mixtures together to create a marbled effect.

Bake for approximately 1 hour until the brownie appears to be set on top. It will still be quite moist and fudgy if checked in the centre with a skewer. Allow to cool at least 2 hours in the tin before carefully lifting out, then slice and dust with icing sugar.

Dutch Speculaas

A family favourite, these are just like bought windmill biscuits.
They make a lovely Christmas gift. You can buy mixes of speculaas spice
in specialist Dutch shops, but it is very easy to make your own.

Makes 36

For the spice mix
2 tablespoons ground cinnamon
2 tablespoons ground cloves
2 tablespoons ground nutmeg
1 teaspoon ground white pepper
1 teaspoon salt

For the biscuits
2¾ cups self-raising flour
2½ tablespoons spice mix
½ cup sugar
½ cup soft brown sugar
250 g butter, cut into cubes
80 ml milk, warmed
½ teaspoon baking soda

Preheat the oven to 160°C. Line two oven trays with non-stick baking paper or silicone sheets.

To make the spice mix, place all the ingredients in an airtight screw-top jar and shake to combine. Store in the pantry.

To make the biscuits, place the self-raising flour, 2½ tablespoons of the spice mix, sugars and butter in a food processor and run the machine until the mixture resembles breadcrumbs. Mix the warm milk and soda together then add to the flour mixture. Pulse the machine to lightly incorporate them into the mixture.

Remove from the food processor bowl and knead lightly to form a smooth, elastic but quite firm dough. Flatten and wrap in cling film and chill in the fridge for 30 minutes.

Roll out to 5 cm thick and cut shapes with a cookie cutter or, if you have a speculaas mould, dust the mould with cornflour and press the mixture in. Turn the mould over and bang down on it to release the biscuits. Arrange on the prepared trays, allowing room to spread. Bake for 15–20 minutes until golden brown. Cool on a wire rack and store in an airtight container.

Wholemeal Ginger Crunch

Makes 24 pieces

For the base
150 g butter
2 tablespoons golden syrup
¾ cup brown sugar
¾ cup long-thread coconut
1½ cups rolled oats
¾ cup wholemeal flour
2 teaspoons baking powder
3 teaspoons ground ginger
1 cup chopped crystallised ginger

For the topping
100 g butter
6 tablespoons golden syrup
2¼ cups icing sugar
3 teaspoons ground ginger

Preheat the oven to 180°C. Line a 20 cm x 30 cm slice tin with non-stick baking paper.

To make the base, melt the butter, golden syrup and sugar together in a large saucepan. Mix in the other ingredients and press the mixture into the prepared tin. Bake for 20 minutes.

To make the topping, melt the butter and golden syrup together and beat in the icing sugar and ginger.

Remove base from the oven and spread the prepared topping over the warm slice. Chill before cutting into 24 pieces.

Orange Manuka Honey Biscuits

These biscuits are gluten free, but you won't be able to tell! I love the flavour of manuka honey but the real delight of these biscuits is their delicious chewiness. Cooked any longer, they become very crisp, but that's not a bad thing either.

Makes 20

2 cups ground pecans (you can use walnuts or almonds for a change)
1 cup caster sugar
grated rind of 1 orange
2 egg whites, beaten to soft peaks
1 tablespoon manuka honey, warmed
icing sugar to dust (about ½ cup)

Preheat the oven to 160°C. Line two baking trays with non-stick baking paper or silicone sheets.

Mix the ground pecans, caster sugar and orange rind together then add the beaten egg white and honey. Scoop up small balls of the mixture and roll them in icing sugar to coat well. Press them flat on the trays, allowing a bit of room to spread out.

Bake for 15–18 minutes and cool on a wire rack. Dust with icing sugar.

Cook School Tips

- *The best thing about these biscuits is they are really forgiving. If you leave them in the oven a bit too long they just become crunchy! Try making tiny ones, and half-dip them in chocolate to serve with coffee.*
- *As this is a gluten-free recipe, make sure you use a gluten-free icing sugar to dust. Some icing sugars have fillers containing gluten in them to stop the sugar clumping, so read the packet carefully!*
- *While it is very easy to make a batch and then watch friends and family gobble them up, these biscuits freeze and defrost well, making the perfect just-in-case option for spontaneous hostessing and unexpected guests.*

This **looks spectacular as a cake presentation** but it can be a bit tricky to cut. However, the toffee topping softens after a few days as long as it hasn't been picked off by passers-by! I have adapted this recipe from something I found in the archives of the Oxford Museum.

Seagars Christmas Cake with Toffee Fruit and Nut Topping

For the cake

1 cup orange juice

250 g butter

1 tablespoon cider vinegar

1 kg mixed dried fruit

1 cup (1 packet) red glacé cherries

1 cup (1 packet) green glacé cherries

1 cup (1 packet) mixed citrus peel

½ cup crystallised ginger, chopped

5 teaspoons mixed spice

1 x 400 g can sweetened condensed milk

1 teaspoon baking soda

2 teaspoons vanilla essence

½ cup Cointreau, Grand Marnier or brandy

2½ cups self-raising flour

For the fruit and nut topping

1 cup mixed nuts: brazils, pecans, almonds, walnuts

1 cup (1 packet) red glacé cherries

1 cup (1 packet) green glacé cherries

2 cups sugar

½ cup water

Preheat the oven to 150°C. Line the base of a 23 cm square spring-form tin with non-stick baking paper and spray the sides with baking spray.

To make the cake, place the orange juice, butter, cider vinegar, mixed fruit, cherries, peel and ginger in a large saucepan and bring to the boil. Remove from heat and stir in the spice, condensed milk, baking soda and vanilla. Add half the liquor and the self-raising flour. Mix well.

Transfer the mixture to the prepared tin and smooth the surface. Bake for 1 hour then turn the temperature down to 140°C and bake a further 1–1½ hours until firm in the centre and deep golden brown.

Remove from the oven and pour over the remaining liquor. Cool in the tin then unclip the sides and remove the cake. Wrap in baking paper and tinfoil, and store in a cool place. This cake can also be eaten straight away.

To make the topping, arrange the nuts and cherries over the top of the cake. Place the sugar and water in a small non-stick saucepan and bring to the boil slowly, just swirling, not stirring. Once the sugar has dissolved, boil rapidly, giving the occasional swirl but avoiding stirring. As the colour changes, watch carefully as the syrup can burn quickly. When it is a good golden syrup colour, carefully drizzle it over the fruit and nuts, letting it drip down the sides of the cake. Cool and set. Store in an airtight cake tin.

The quaint old-fashioned
tradition of afternoon tea can
actually move with the times.

Lemon Passionfruit Roulade

For the roulade
½ cup caster sugar, plus extra to dust
3 eggs, at room temperature
½ cup self-raising flour

For the filling
300 ml cream
½ cup lemon passionfruit curd

Preheat the oven to 200°C. Spray and line a large 25 cm x 35 cm sponge roll tin with non-stick baking paper. Spray the paper lightly with baking spray.

To make the roulade, place the sugar in a mixing bowl then break in the eggs and beat with an electric mixer until thick, pale and fluffy. Sift the flour and fold into the egg mixture. Spread into the prepared tin and bake for 7–8 minutes until it is pale gold and the cake pulls away from the sides of the tin.

Turn out onto a fresh sheet of paper (can be greaseproof or waxed paper) and cool completely. Score a line 2 cm from the long edge of the cake.

To make the filling, whip the cream until thick then fold in the lemon passionfruit curd, which will thicken the cream a little more. Spread evenly over the cake and roll up from the long edge, using the paper to keep the roll tight, as for sushi. Dust with extra caster sugar or icing sugar.

Lemon Passionfruit Curd

Makes about 2½ cups

½ cup passionfruit pulp (4–5 fruit)
grated rind and juice of 5 lemons
6 egg yolks

1 cup sugar
200 g butter, cubed

Whisk all ingredients together and keep whisking over medium to high heat until the mixture thickens and is well combined. Do not boil. Cool before storing in the fridge.

*The **aromatic sweetness** of passionfruit is always a winner in the **sweets stakes**!*

Rhubarb Streusel Cake

So moist it can easily be served as a dessert or for a special afternoon tea or supper, streusel cake is best eaten with a fork.

For the streusel topping
½ teaspoon ground cinnamon
½ cup flour
75 g butter, cubed
3 tablespoons caster sugar

For the cake
1 bunch rhubarb stalks (about 6),
chopped into small pieces —
don't include any leaf as it is toxic
½ cup caster sugar
100 g butter, softened
2 eggs
¾ cup self-raising flour
2 tablespoons milk
icing sugar to dust

Preheat the oven to 180°C. Spray a 21 cm spring-form tin with baking spray and line with non-stick baking paper.

To make the streusel topping, mix all ingredients in a food processor until they resemble breadcrumbs. Set aside until required.

To make the cake, mix chopped rhubarb with 1 tablespoon of the caster sugar, tossing well, then set aside. Beat the butter and remaining caster sugar until light and fluffy. Add the eggs one at a time, beating after each one is added. Mix in the flour and milk to form a soft, pourable consistency. Spread into the prepared tin. Cover with rhubarb and then sprinkle the streusel topping over this. Bake for 1¼ hours until the cake is golden brown and pulling away from the edges of the tin. Test with a skewer to check the centre is cooked. Cool on a wire rack in the tin. Dust with icing sugar and add a dollop of cream to serve.

Chardonnay Cake

**Perfect for wine lovers, this makes a large cake. Serve it with a glass
of Chardonnay, of course.**

1¾ cups flour
1 teaspoon baking powder
1 teaspoon salt
½ teaspoon baking soda
1 cup caster sugar
100 g butter, softened
3 tablespoons extra-virgin olive oil
2 eggs
grated rind of 1 lemon
grated rind of 1 orange
1 teaspoon vanilla essence
250 ml chardonnay
2 cups small grapes (ideally chardonnay, seedless if possible)
50 g melted butter
4 tablespoons sugar

Preheat the oven to 200°C. Spray a 23–25 cm spring-form tin with baking spray
and line with non-stick baking paper.

Mix the flour, baking powder, salt and baking soda in a large bowl. In a
separate bowl, beat the caster sugar, butter and olive oil until smooth. Add the
eggs, lemon and orange rind and vanilla. Add the flour mixture alternately with
the wine in three additions. Pour the batter into the prepared tin and sprinkle
the grapes on top. Bake for 20–25 minutes until the top is just set. Brush gently
with the melted butter and sprinkle the sugar on top. Return to the oven for a
further 20–25 minutes, until a skewer inserted in the centre comes out clean.
Cool in the tin on a wire rack. Serve at room temperature with softly whipped
cream and fresh grapes.

Nectarine and Plum Cake

This is a lovely afternoon-tea cake or delicious for dessert with a dollop of
cream or thick yoghurt.

4 plums, halved and stoned
4 nectarines, sliced off the stone
1 tablespoon caster sugar
1 tablespoon ground cinnamon
200 g butter
1½ cups sugar
3 eggs
1½ cups flour
1½ teaspoons baking powder
icing sugar to dust

Preheat the oven to 180°C. Spray a 23 cm spring-form tin with baking spray and
line with non-stick baking paper.

Mix the fruit in a bowl and sprinkle with the caster sugar and cinnamon. In
a separate bowl, beat the butter and sugar together then beat in the eggs, one
at a time. Mix in the flour and baking powder. Pour into the prepared tin and
arrange the fruit over the top of the batter.

Bake for approximately 1 hour and 15 minutes until the cake is golden and
pulling away from the sides of the tin. Cool in the tin on a wire rack. Carefully
transfer to a cake plate and dust with icing sugar to serve.

Lemon Raisin Bars

Makes 16 bars

For the base
1 cup self-raising flour
¾ cup rolled oats
100 g butter, cubed
½ cup soft brown sugar
1 teaspoon mixed spice

For the topping
50 g butter, melted
4 eggs
1 cup soft brown sugar
1 cup raisins
¾ cup dessicated coconut
grated rind and juice of 1 lemon

For the icing
grated rind and juice of 1 lemon
1 cup icing sugar

Preheat the oven to 180°C. Spray a 20 cm x 30 cm sponge roll tin with baking spray and line with non-stick baking paper.

To make the base, mix all the ingredients together in a food processor until the mixture sticks in a ball. Press into the prepared tin and bake for 12 minutes.

To make the topping, beat the butter, eggs and brown sugar together. Add the raisins, coconut and lemon rind and juice. Pour over the warm base and return to the oven for 20–25 minutes until the topping is set and pale golden brown. Mark into pieces and allow to cool in the tin.

To make the icing, mix the lemon rind and juice with the icing sugar to form a smooth, runny icing. Drizzle this over the cooled bars and allow to set. Store in an airtight container.

Farmhouse Coconut Crispies

These gluten-free crispies are perfect with a cuppa, especially if you
dunk them!

Makes 36–40

½ cup caster sugar
2 eggs, separated
1 cup dessicated coconut
1 teaspoon coconut essence

Preheat the oven to 150°C. Line two oven trays with non-stick baking paper.

Beat the sugar and egg yolks until pale and thick. Mix in the coconut and
essence. In a separate bowl, beat the egg whites until stiff and then fold into the
coconut mixture.

Place teaspoonfuls of mixture on the trays, leaving plenty of room to spread.
Bake for 15 minutes then reduce heat to 110°C and bake a further 15 minutes.
Cool on a wire rack and store in an airtight container.

Cook School Tips for Baking Biscuits

- *Make it hot. If you are cooking biscuits, always put them in a preheated
oven. However, the baking trays should be cold so the biscuits keep
their shape. Place the trays in the middle of the oven to make sure the
biscuits are cooked as evenly as possible or, better still, always use fan-
bake. A biscuit is cooked when it is pale golden underneath.*
- *Wrap the dough. If you need to roll out dough, it is much easier if
you place it between two sheets of baking paper or cling film. This
eliminates the need for extra flour and reduces handling, giving a
lighter result.*
- *Use a wet fork. Before using a fork to press down biscuit dough, dip it in
cold water to keep it from sticking. Re-dip in water as required.*

Cashew and White Chocolate Blondie

Makes 16 pieces

For the blondie
150 g butter
1 cup brown sugar, firmly packed
2 eggs
2 teaspoons vanilla essence
1¾ cups flour
1 teaspoon baking powder
½ cup white chocolate buttons, chopped
½ cup cashew nuts (I use roasted salted cashews)
½ cup fudge bits (cut up a packet of caramels or use scraps of Russian fudge)

For the icing
100 g white chocolate buttons
50 g butter
1 cup icing sugar
milk to mix

Preheat the oven to 180°C. Spray a 20 cm square cake tin with baking spray and line with non-stick baking paper or tinfoil. (If using tinfoil, this will need a good spray of baking spray.)

To make the blondie, beat butter and brown sugar together, and add the eggs and vanilla. Mix in all the other ingredients. Transfer to the prepared tin. Bake for 40 minutes. Cool in the tin.

To make the icing, heat the white chocolate and butter in the microwave, stirring frequently until melted. Mix in icing sugar and a little milk to make a smooth, thick icing. Spread over the cooled blondie and allow to set before cutting into 16 pieces.

Carrot Cupcakes with Peanut Butter Frosting

Makes 12 cupcakes

For the cupcakes
125 g butter, melted
¾ cup sugar
¼ cup brown sugar
2 eggs
1¼ cups flour
½ teaspoon salt
2 teaspoons mixed spice
1 teaspoon baking powder
250 g (1 cup) grated carrot
½ cup sultanas
½ cup chopped walnuts

For the frosting
50 g butter, softened
½ cup crunchy peanut butter
125 g cream cheese, softened at room temperature
(use traditional — don't substitute softened cream cheese)
2 cups icing sugar
1 handful chopped walnuts

Preheat the oven to 180°C. Line a standard 12-cup muffin tin with paper cupcake liners.

To make the cupcakes, beat the butter, sugars and eggs together. Mix in other ingredients. Divide mixture between the cupcake liners. Bake for 18–20 minutes. Cool in the tin until completely cold.

To make the frosting, beat all the ingredients until smoothly combined. (I use an electric mixer.) Spread on cold cupcakes and sprinkle with chopped walnuts.

Butterscotch Coconut Slice

Makes 20 pieces

For the base
125 g butter, softened to room temperature
½ cup sugar
1 tablespoon golden syrup
2 teaspoons caramel essence
1 cup flour
2 teaspoons baking powder
½ cup long-thread coconut

For the topping
1¼ cups long-thread coconut
1 egg
3 tablespoons sweetened condensed milk
50 g butter, melted
½ teaspoon caramel essence

Preheat the oven to 180°C. Spray a 20 cm x 30 cm slice tin with baking spray and line with non-stick baking paper.

Beat the butter, sugar, golden syrup and caramel essence together. Mix in the flour, baking powder and coconut. Press the mixture into the prepared tin.

Mix the topping ingredients together and spread over the base. Bake for 25–30 minutes until golden brown. Cool in the tin before cutting into pieces.

Chocolate Angel Food Cake with Chocoholics' Sauce

For the cake	For the sauce
½ cup cocoa	250 ml cream
¾ cup caster sugar	1 x 375 g packet dark or milk
1 cup flour	chocolate melts
12–15 egg whites (2 cups)	
¾ cup caster sugar	
1 teaspoon cream of tartar	
¼ teaspoon or pinch of salt	
1 teaspoon vanilla essence	

Preheat the oven to 160°C. To make the cake, sift the cocoa, the first measure of caster sugar and flour together twice to ensure they are aerated and lump free. Set aside.

Place egg whites, cream of tartar and salt in a large bowl, preferably metal, glass or china, not plastic. Using an electric beater, beat until soft peaks form. Gradually add the second measure of caster sugar and beat until the mixture is thick and glossy. Turn the beater to low speed and add the vanilla, then slowly mix or fold in the sifted flour, cocoa and sugar. Spoon into the tin and bang it down a couple of times on the bench to remove any air pockets.

Bake for 40–45 minutes until the cake is quite dry and cracked on the surface. Remove from the oven and turn upside down to rest and cool in the tin. It is very important to cool it upside down. When quite cold, turn a knife around the edge of the tin and the central tube. Remove the tin and lift off the base.

To make the sauce, place cream and chocolate melts into a small saucepan and gently heat, stirring to combine well. The sauce will set solid in the fridge and needs to be warmed to serve. It will keep covered in the fridge for 3–4 weeks.

Cut the cake with a serrated knife and serve with chocolate sauce, cream or ice cream.

See Angel Inspirations and Cook School Tips over the page

Angel food cake is fat-free. If it's served with berries or a fruit sauce it fits into the **not-so-bad-for-you category.** *It makes a perfect end to Christmas dinner.* For this to work, you must have an angel food cake tin — do not *spray or grease it in any way.* Do not *line it with baking paper.*

Angel Inspirations

- Make a confetti cake by folding hundreds and thousands through at the last stage. Children will love it.

- Cut the cake horizontally into thin slices and layer with frosting, whipped cream or mousse for an impressive celebration cake.

- Pour strong espresso coffee over the cake and serve with good vanilla ice cream for an affogato-style dessert.

- Toast leftovers the next day for breakfast and serve with lemon curd and berries. You can also grill slices on the barbecue.

- Use it as a base for summer pudding, tiramisu or trifle.

- Make lovely lamingtons by cutting it into squares and rolling in icing and then coconut.

- Angel food cake makes a lovely alternative to traditional wedding cake, frosted with vanilla or orange liqueur frosting and decorated with ribbons and rose petals.

- Using gluten-free flour, I've also found it makes an excellent gluten-free dessert.

Cook School Tips for Baking Angels

An angel food cake is really just a pavlova with a wee bit of flour. It is one of those cakes you can always make because it has simple ingredients you can easily find in your cupboards or at the dairy down the road. It is also incredibly versatile and can be altered to suit pretty much any occasion. If there are any, leftovers are great too.

- I am not big on sifting, and never do it unless I have to. Angel food cakes and sponges are have-to occasions. The flour and sugar have to be sifted together twice to aerate them — that's what makes the cake so light and airy. I sift onto baking paper or a silicone sheet, then pull the edges together, pour it back into the sieve and start again.

- If you don't have an angel food cake tin you can use a high-sided spring-form tin with a glass placed in the middle, but for best results purchase an angel food cake tin — it has little legs on the top to stand on when you invert the cake to cool.

- It is really important never to grease an angel food cake tin. The cake is completely fat-free and greasing the tin would upset the chemistry.

- When it has finished cooking, you need to invert the tin to let gravity help stabilise the cake's height. It will sink like a soufflé if you leave out this step.

- This cake freezes very well so is perfect to whip up then hide away for those unexpected entertaining occasions. Freeze it stored in a plastic box to stop it being squashed in the depths of the freezer.

Aunty Peg's Ginger Gems

This is Carol from Stratford's Aunty Peg's recipe and it's a winner.
Gem irons used to be quite difficult to buy, but don't be deterred. We have
found a supplier for our kitchen store and you can often find them in junk
shops or at garage sales.

Makes 20–24

50 g butter
2 tablespoons golden syrup
½ cup milk, at room temperature
1 egg, at room temperature
½ cup sugar
1 cup flour
3 teaspoons ground ginger
1 teaspoon baking soda
whipped cream to fill
icing sugar to dust

Preheat the oven to 200°C. Place gem irons in the oven to heat.

Place butter and golden syrup in a small saucepan and warm to melt the
butter. Beat the milk and egg together in a mixing bowl, add the butter and
golden syrup mixture then mix in the dry ingredients.

Spray the hot gem iron with baking spray and spoon in the mixture to three-
quarter fill the irons. Cook for 12–15 minutes. Turn out and cool on a wire rack.
Split the cooked gems, fill with whipped cream and top with a dusting of icing
sugar. Alternatively, they can be buttered.

*A pinch of panache and
a dash of nostalgia.*

Coffee Kisses

These are lovely light gluten-free biscuits, with a great sweet kick.

Makes 36

---

4 egg whites
2 tablespoons caster sugar
2 cups icing sugar
2 tablespoons sweetened coffee and chicory essence
1¼ cups ground almonds
2 tablespoons maize cornflour
1 cup white chocolate melts, melted

Preheat the oven to 160°C. Line two oven trays with non-stick baking paper or silicone sheets.

In an electric mixer fitted with a whisk attachment, beat the egg whites until stiff. While continuing to beat, slowly add the caster sugar and icing sugar, just a spoonful at a time, until it is all incorporated. Add the coffee essence, then the ground almonds and cornflour. Place dessertspoonfuls of the mixture on the prepared trays and bake for 18–20 minutes until crisp and dry. Don't open the oven door too often while they are cooking.

Cool on a wire rack. When completely cold, sandwich together with melted white chocolate.

Emily's Lemon Shortcake

Emily is our wonderful new cooking teacher at Seagars.
Her children's workshops are particularly popular.

Makes 24

For the shortcake
1 cup self-raising flour
1 cup flour
pinch of salt
1 cup sugar
100 g cold butter, grated
1 egg, beaten
2 tablespoons milk
icing sugar to dust

For the filling
100 g butter
grated rind and juice of 3 lemons
1 cup sugar
3 eggs, beaten

Preheat the oven to 180°C. Line a 20 cm x 30 cm slice tin with non-stick baking paper.

To make the shortcake, mix the flours, salt and sugar together. Rub in the grated butter. Add the beaten egg and milk and mix until it forms a dough. Divide off one-third of the dough, wrap in cling film and chill in the fridge. Press the remaining dough into the lined tin and bake for 8–10 minutes until pale and just cooked.

While the shortcake is cooking, make the filling. Place the butter in a saucepan over low heat with the lemon rind and juice and sugar. Stir until the sugar is dissolved. Add the beaten eggs and continue to stir until it starts to thicken. Do not let it boil. Pour the lemon filling over the partially cooked shortcake.

Cut walnut-sized pieces of the refrigerated dough and place all over the lemon filling. When cooked this will look like a patchwork crumble with two-thirds of the topping under the filling and one-third on the top. Bake for a further 10–15 minutes until the shortcake is lightly golden brown. Cool in the tin and cut into squares. Dust with icing sugar to serve.

Cook School Tips for Gluten-free Cooking

More and more people are eating gluten-free foods for either health or lifestyle reasons. While there are many foods that are already naturally gluten free, you can also adapt many recipes to make them gluten free. Here are some tried-and-true tricks to help you.

- If you want to thicken a sauce, replace every tablespoon of wheaten flour, with one of the following:

  - 1½ teaspoons maize cornflour
  - 1½ teaspoons arrowroot
  - 1½ teaspoons potato starch
  - 1 tablespoon white or brown rice flour
  - 2 teaspoons tapioca flour

- If you want to modify a baking recipe to make it gluten free, replace every cup of wheat flour with one of the following:

  - 1 cup maize cornflour
  - 1 cup rice flour
  - 1 cup fine cornmeal
  - ½ cup rice flour and ½ cup soy flour
  - ½ cup rice flour and ½ cup maize cornflour
  - ½ cup maize cornflour and 1 tablespoon ground millet
  - ½ cup soy flour and ½ cup potato flour

- Gluten-free foods lack the flour protein to rise as easily as wheat-based products. To give them a helping hand, mix your raising agent with water before adding the flour. You can make your own gluten-free baking powder by putting ¼ cup baking soda, ½ cup cream of tartar and ¼ cup of arrowroot or potato flour (to prevent clumping) in an airtight container and shaking to combine.

Dark Moist Gingerbread

This is great served as a pudding with custard and cream or as an afternoon tea loaf. It is also good with cheese for a quick breakfast pick-me-up.

Makes 1 standard loaf

2 teaspoons mixed spice
1 teaspoon ground cinnamon
3 teaspoons ground ginger
2½ cups flour
1 teaspoon baking powder
100 g butter
2 tablespoons golden syrup
1 tablespoon molasses
¾ cup brown sugar
1 cup milk
2 teaspoons baking soda
½ cup chopped crystallised ginger

Preheat the oven to 180°C. Spray a 12 cm x 23 cm loaf tin with baking spray and line with non-stick baking paper.

Place the spices, flour and baking powder in a bowl. Gently heat the butter, golden syrup, molasses and brown sugar together. Stir until the butter is melted. Add the milk and then mix in the baking soda before stirring into the other dry ingredients. Add the chopped ginger and mix really well.

Pour into the prepared tin and bake for 45–50 minutes. Cool in the tin for 10 minutes then turn out onto a wire rack to cool completely. Serve in chunky slices.

Café-style Friands

We make this mixture at the café and store it in a covered container in the
fridge to make friands as required. The mixture will keep this way
for up to 10 days.

Makes 30–36 friands

Master Recipe

2 cups sugar
1¼ cups flour or gluten-free flour
1½ cups ground almonds
300 g butter, melted
10 egg whites
flavour or fruit of your choice (see page 146)

Mix the sugar, almonds, flour, butter and egg whites together and cool in the
fridge for at least 20 minutes before using.

Preheat the oven to 200°C. Spray a 12-cup friand mould or standard 12-cup
muffin tin with baking spray.

Spoon a tablespoon of friand mixture into each mould or cup. Add the flavour
or fruit of your choice and spoon a second tablespoon of mixture into the
moulds or cups. The fruit will cook and sink to the bottom of the friands.

Bake for 18–25 minutes, until the friands are well risen, golden and firm
when gently pressed in the centre. Cool for 5 minutes in the mould or tin before
carefully turning out to cool on a wire rack.

See Friand Inspirations over the page

Friand Inspirations

The following flavour variations make enough each for 12 friands

Blueberry and Lemon Friands

1 cup fresh or frozen blueberries (do not thaw)
¼ cup lemon curd
lemon zest to garnish

Follow the master recipe, dividing the blueberries between 12 friands and adding a teaspoonful of lemon curd to each before covering with the second portion of friand mixture. Garnish with fresh lemon zest.

Raspberry and Coconut Friands

1 cup fresh or frozen raspberries (do not thaw)
¼ cup long-thread coconut
long-thread coconut to garnish

Follow the master recipe, dividing the raspberries between the 12 friands and topping with pinches of coconut before covering with the second portion of friand mixture. Garnish with extra coconut threads.

Cinnamon Peach Friands

2 fresh peaches, stones removed, chopped into small pieces
1 teaspoon ground cinnamon
1 tablespoon caster sugar
icing sugar to dust

Follow the master recipe. Mix the chopped peaches with the cinnamon and caster sugar. Divide the peach mixture between the friands before covering with the second portion of friand mixture. Dust with icing sugar.

Coconut Lime Drizzle Cake

This is an excellent cake to serve warm with tropical fruit or strawberries
as a dessert.

Makes 20–25 pieces

For the cake
2 cups long-thread coconut
2 cups self-raising flour
2 cups sugar
2 cups milk
2 teaspoons vanilla essence

For the topping
grated rind and juice of 3 limes
1½ cups icing sugar

Preheat the oven to 180°C. Spray a 20 cm x 30 cm slice tin with baking spray
and line with non-stick baking paper.

Mix the cake ingredients together in a bowl until well combined. Pour into the
prepared tin and bake for 35–40 minutes. Remove from the oven and stand the
tin on a wire rack to cool.

Mix the lime rind and juice and icing sugar together to make a thin, runny
icing. Drizzle icing over the warm cake and cool in the tin. Set the icing in the
fridge before cutting the cake into pieces. Top with lime zest if you like.

4. The Main Event

Find a grace or wee tradition for your family to share when you eat together. This is one of our favourites:

Bless O Lord before we dine

Each dish of food, each cup of wine

And bless our hearts, that we may be

Very thankful of what we owe to thee

Pecan and Panko-crusted Chicken

Panko is Japanese rice-flour breadcrumbs. Look for them in the Asian section
of the supermarket. At a push you can use conventional dry breadcrumbs but
they are not nearly as good.

Serves 4

4 single skinless and boneless chicken breasts
salt and freshly ground black pepper
1 cup panko breadcrumbs
1 cup finely chopped pecans
50 g butter, melted
3 tablespoons oil
50 g butter
¼ cup finely chopped shallots
¾ cup chicken stock
2 tablespoons chopped parsley

Preheat the oven to 200°C.

Sprinkle the chicken with salt and pepper. Mix the panko and pecans in a
shallow dish. Brush both sides of the chicken with the melted butter then roll in
the panko mixture.

Heat oil in a medium-sized non-stick ovenproof frypan and fry the chicken on
both sides for a couple of minutes until browned. Place the pan in the oven and
cook for 15–18 minutes until the chicken is cooked through.

Remove chicken from the pan and keep warm. Wipe out any crumbs from
the pan and heat the second measure of butter. Add the shallots to soften for
2 minutes. Add the stock and parsley and simmer for 2–3 minutes. Season as
desired and pour over the chicken. Serve with roasted potatoes and greens of
your choice.

Salmon, Leek and Baby-pea Parcels

If you are cutting the salmon into pieces yourself, make each piece about
the size of a Weet-Bix. While salmon seems a little expensive, it is quite oily
and rich and the portions can be small. It's a great source of protein with a
whopping side-order of omega-3 fatty acids.

Serves 2

2 x 140 g salmon fillets (skin on or off)
salt and freshly ground black pepper
1 leek, washed and very thinly sliced
½ cup frozen baby peas
4 heaped teaspoons crème fraîche, plus extra to serve
2 tablespoons chopped parsley

Preheat the oven to 200°C (unless you'd rather microwave). Cut two 40–50 cm
squares of baking (not greaseproof) paper. Season fillets as desired and place each
fillet in the middle of a paper square. Top each with half the leek, peas and crème
fraîche. Sprinkle with chopped parsley and more salt and pepper, if desired.

Fold up the parcels and place in an ovenproof or microwaveproof dish. Bake
for 15 minutes or microwave on full power for 4–5 minutes. Place contents of
the parcels on warmed plates and add extra spoonfuls of crème fraîche to serve.

See Salmon and Leek Parcel Inspirations over the page

Salmon and Leek Parcel Inspirations

- If you want to make the parcels a little lighter, use lite crème fraîche or sour cream, but you do need something liquid to create steam inside the parcels and to create a sauce for your salmon and vegetables.

- As long as they are chopped small, you can use any vegetables in the parcel. Instead of leeks and peas, you could add grated carrot or pumpkin, sliced asparagus or chopped Asian greens and pickled ginger garnished with shredded nori to serve.

- You can use any firm-fleshed fish in the parcels. Try white fish with olives, tomatoes and peppers.

- When you close the parcels, make sure they aren't too tight. They are supposed to work as miniature steam ovens and need room around the fish for the steam to build up.

- Serve the contents of the parcels on mashed potatoes, roasted vegetables or brown rice.

- If you are making this for a dinner party, serve the parcels as they come from the oven so your guests can open up their own wee gift at the table.

- You can make more parcels than you require and freeze them uncooked.

Salmon, Bok Choy and Asparagus Salad with Sesame Ginger Dressing

Bok choy works well with the Asian-flavoured dressing, but you can use
baby spinach or mesclun, if preferred.

Serves 4

For the salmon marinade
4 x 160 g salmon fillets,
skinned and boned
⅓ cup soy sauce
2 teaspoons grated ginger
2 teaspoons caster sugar
juice of ½ lemon

For the dressing
⅓ cup olive oil
1 tablespoon sesame oil
2 tablespoons sweet chilli sauce
1 tablespoon rice vinegar
1 teaspoon finely grated fresh ginger
grated rind and juice of 2 limes

For the salad
2 bunches asparagus, trimmed and sliced
2 handfuls baby bok choy leaves
1 bunch coriander leaves, chopped
2 stalks celery, including leaves,
thinly sliced

To marinate the salmon, place it in a shallow dish, checking carefully there are no
bones. Mix soy, ginger, sugar and lemon juice and pour over the salmon to coat.
Cover and put in the fridge for about 30 minutes, but no longer than 1 hour.

Preheat the oven to 200°C. Remove salmon from the marinade and bake or grill
the fish for about 8 minutes, until it is nicely coloured but still pink in the middle.

To make the dressing, put all the dressing ingredients in a screw-top jar and
shake to combine.

To prepare the salad, heat a small saucepan of water to boiling. Toss in the
asparagus and cook for 3 minutes, then drain. Divide the hot asparagus, bok
choy, coriander and celery between 4 plates. Top with the salmon and drizzle the
dressing over.

*Great produce and a simple
recipe are what make the best
dishes — and it takes confidence
to realise that.*

Rocket and Feta-Stuffed Chicken Breasts with Sweet Chilli Yoghurt Sauce

Serves 10

For the chicken

10 boneless chicken breasts, skin on
1 cup roughly chopped rocket leaves
300 g feta cheese, crumbled or chopped
1 teaspoon freshly ground black pepper
1 cup sour cream
2–3 cloves garlic, crushed (1 teaspoon)
10 rashers rindless streaky bacon
garlic salt

For the sauce

500 ml thick natural yoghurt
1 cup chopped parsley
1–2 cloves garlic, crushed (½ teaspoon)
½ cup sweet chilli sauce

Preheat the oven to 200°C.

To prepare the chicken, cut a pocket in the underside of each breast. Place the rocket, feta, pepper, sour cream and garlic in a food processor and pulse the machine to form a thick paste. Spoon the paste into the pockets on the underside of each breast and wrap a bacon rasher around each, like a bandage. Place in a large roasting dish and sprinkle with garlic salt. Roast for 25–30 minutes until the bacon and chicken skin are crispy and the chicken is cooked through.

To make the yoghurt sauce, mix all the ingredients together and keep covered in the fridge. Serve at room temperature over the hot chicken breasts or in a separate bowl as an accompaniment.

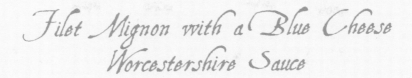

Filet Mignon with a Blue Cheese Worcestershire Sauce

Blue Castello is a soft cheese made from cow's milk. It's hard to resist in this special-occasion fillet.

Serves 6

For the fillets

150 g Blue Castello cheese
6 individual eye fillet steaks
6 rashers rindless streaky bacon

For the sauce

150 g Blue Castello cheese
150 ml cream
¼ cup Worcestershire sauce
125 g cream cheese
salt and freshly ground black pepper

To prepare the fillets, cut the cheese into six pieces. Make a cut in the side of each fillet and insert a piece of the cheese, wrap with a bacon rasher and secure with a skewer. Heat a frypan or barbecue plate until sizzling. Cook steaks for 2 minutes without disturbing them, then turn over and cook for 2 more minutes. Remove from heat and cover with a tent of tinfoil. Rest the meat for at least 10–15 minutes in a warming drawer. (You can rest it for longer if time and organisation permit.)

To make the sauce, place all the ingredients in a small saucepan and whisk until bubbling and smoothly combined. Season as desired, ladle onto serving plate or plates and place fillets on top.

Thai Chicken Pies

Serves 6

4 tablespoons Thai green curry paste
6 skinless and boneless chicken breasts, cut into bite-sized chunks
2 cups sliced button mushrooms
2 red capsicums, deseeded and chopped
2 cups peeled and diced pumpkin, potato or kumara (cut into 1 cm cubes)
1 tablespoon oil
grated rind and juice of 2 limes
1 tablespoon Asian fish sauce
250 ml chicken stock
2 tablespoons cornflour
1 x 400 g can coconut cream
1 bunch coriander leaves, chopped
1 cup frozen baby peas
6 sheets frozen flaky pastry, thawed
1 egg yolk
1 teaspoon water

Mix curry paste with the chicken, mushrooms, capsicums and pumpkin, potato or kumara. Cover and marinate for 1 hour in the fridge.

Heat oil in a large frypan and fry the chicken and vegetables for 5 minutes, stirring. Add the lime rind and juice, fish sauce, chicken stock, cornflour and coconut cream and cook for 5 more minutes. Remove from heat and stir in coriander and peas. Set aside to cool.

Preheat the oven to 220°C. Spray six 1-cup ramekins with baking spray.

Divide the curry mixture between the ramekins. Fold each sheet of pastry in half then roll out and cut 6 circles of pastry a centimetre or so bigger than the ramekins. Whisk the egg yolk and water together and brush some of the egg wash around the rim of the ramekins. Drape pastry over the ramekins and press down over the edge. Brush the surface of each pie with the egg wash. Bake for 25–30 minutes until puffed and golden and the filling is piping hot.

Salt 'n' Pepper Calamari and Prawns

Serves 6

1 tablespoon ground Szechuan peppercorns
1 teaspoon dried chilli flakes
2 tablespoons sea salt flakes
1 teaspoon five spice powder
½ cup rice flour (or ¼ cup flour and ¼ cup cornflour)
6 squid tubes, cleaned and cut into chunks
1 kg green prawns, peeled and deveined
vegetable oil to deep fry
lemon wedges to serve

Place the pepper, chilli, salt, five spice powder and flour in a food processor and run the machine to chop finely and mix really well.

Score the squid pieces diagonally with a small sharp knife. Toss squid and prawns in the flour mixture to coat well.

Heat oil in a large wok or frypan and deep fry the calamari and prawns in batches for 1–2 minutes until just cooked through. Keep warm as you cook the remainder. Serve immediately with lemon wedges and a green salad.

Artichoke and Chicken Salad with Croutons

Serves 4–6

For the dressing	For the salad
1 cup oil (rice bran or canola)	1 cold roasted chicken
¼ cup white wine vinegar	2 cups oven-dried tomatoes or
grated rind and juice of 1 orange	semi-dried tomatoes (available in
1 teaspoon Dijon mustard	the supermarket deli section)
1 teaspoon tomato sauce	1 x 400 g can artichoke hearts in
salt and freshly ground black pepper	brine, drained
	1 loaf ciabatta, sourdough or
	other rustic bread
	½ cup extra-virgin olive oil
	½ teaspoon garlic salt
	1 bag mixed salad leaves
	(rocket, mesclun, etc)
	½ cup chopped or snipped fresh herbs

To make the dressing, place all the ingredients in a screw-top squeezy bottle and shake to combine. Store in the fridge.

Preheat the oven to 200°C. To prepare the salad, remove all chicken meat from the bones, reserving them for the stockpot. Chop up the tomatoes and artichokes. Break up the bread into rustic bite-sized croutons. Mix the bread with olive oil and garlic salt and spread out in a single layer in a roasting dish. Bake for 20–25 minutes, watching carefully so they don't burn, and tossing and stirring to toast evenly. Toss the chicken, tomato, artichokes, croutons, salad leaves and herbs in a large bowl or on a platter. Drizzle the dressing over and serve immediately.

Peasant-style Balsamic Chicken with White Beans

This is yummy as is but, for a change, you can make it more stew-like by adding a cup of good chicken stock and warming through to wilt the greens and heat the beans.

Serves 4

750 g skinless chicken thighs
salt and freshly ground black pepper
2–3 cloves garlic, crushed (1 teaspoon)
2 tablespoons grainy mustard
3 tablespoons balsamic vinegar
1 x 400 g can cannellini beans, drained and rinsed
2 cups cherry tomatoes, halved
1 cup cubed feta cheese
2 handfuls baby rocket or spinach leaves
2 tablespoons extra-virgin olive oil
3 lemons, cut into wedges to serve

Season chicken as desired. Whisk garlic, mustard and balsamic together and pour over chicken. Toss to coat well. Cover and place in the fridge for 30 minutes.

Preheat the barbecue plate or a frypan and cook chicken for about 10 minutes until cooked through and browned. Slice chicken into a bowl. Toss with the beans, cherry tomatoes, feta, salad leaves and oil. Serve with lemon wedges to squeeze over.

Bourbon Pork Ribs

These are messy to eat so have a big basket of mopping-up bread and lots of paper napkins or moistened face flannels ready and tuck in! You'll need to discreetly pass around the toothpicks at the end.

Serves 4–8

2–3 kg pork ribs (these can be large as long as they
fit into a big saucepan)
½ cup brown sugar
½ cup tomato sauce
1 cup bourbon
½ cup cider vinegar
¼ cup Worcestershire sauce
¼ cup soy sauce
1 x 400 g can tomatoes in juice, puréed in a blender
1 teaspoon freshly ground black pepper

Cover ribs with water and bring to the boil. Simmer for 10 minutes then cool in the water. Drain and pat dry with paper towels.

To make the marinade, whisk the remaining ingredients together in a bowl until well combined. Pour over the cooled ribs. Cover the dish and marinate in the fridge overnight or longer — 24 hours is ideal.

Heat the barbecue grill or preheat the oven to 180°C. Cook the ribs in the marinade for 25–35 minutes, turning to cook evenly. Slice into smaller rib portions before serving. Pile on a plate and serve with baked potatoes and sweetcorn.

Cook School Tip

The longer the meat marinates, the more flavoursome and tender the ribs will be. Two hours is a minimum, but 24 hours is ideal.

Chicken Margarita

My friend Deborah (Lady Mills) and I have adopted Santa Margarita
as our patron saint. Certainly, we love sharing her cocktails
and they would be perfect to have with this dish.

Serves 4

For the marinade

1 tablespoon ground cumin
1 tablespoon ground chilli powder or Mexican chilli powder
grated rind and juice of 3 limes
6–8 cloves garlic, crushed (2 teaspoons)
3 tablespoons olive oil
6–8 chicken pieces (thighs, wings or breasts)

For the sauce

½ cup gold tequila
½ cup water
salt and freshly ground black pepper
½ cup chopped flat-leafed parsley to garnish
1 cup halved cherry tomatoes to garnish

To prepare the marinade, combine cumin, chilli powder, lime rind and juice,
garlic and oil to form a paste. Coat the chicken pieces with the paste. Cover and
place in the fridge to marinate for least 1 hour, but preferably longer.

To make the sauce, heat an ovenproof frypan and cook the chicken pieces
until browned. Scrape any remaining marinade into the pan and add tequila
and water. Cover pan and simmer for 25–30 minutes until the chicken is
cooked through.

Transfer chicken to a serving plate and keep warm while you reduce the liquid
to a coating-consistency sauce. Season sauce as desired and spoon over the
chicken. Garnish with parsley and cherry tomatoes and serve with brown rice
or pasta.

Scandinavian Pork Meatballs with Sour Cream and Dill

You can use lamb or beef mince instead of pork, if preferred.

Serves 4

For the meatballs

2 medium onions, finely chopped
500 g pork mince
1 egg
½ teaspoon salt
½ teaspoon freshly ground black pepper
2 tablespoons chopped dill
1 tablespoon oil

For the sauce

250 g sour cream
½ teaspoon Worcestershire sauce
1 tablespoon grainy mustard
1 tablespoon chopped fresh dill to garnish

To make the meatballs, mix onion, pork, egg, salt, pepper and dill together. Shape into 16–20 meatballs. (I find wearing a pair of disposable gloves is best for this job.)

Heat oil in a non-stick frypan and fry meatballs for 10–12 minutes until golden brown. Drain on paper towels.

To make the sauce, tip out any excess fat from the frypan and add the sour cream, Worcestershire sauce and mustard. Stir to mix well. To serve, pour the warm sauce over the meatballs, sprinkle with dill to garnish and accompany with noodles or mashed potato.

Aubergine and Capsicum Parmigiana with Rich Tomato Sauce

Serves 4–6

For the sauce (makes 3 cups)
25 g butter
2 tablespoons olive oil
2 medium onions, chopped finely
2–3 cloves garlic, crushed (1 teaspoon)
1.5 kg ripe tomatoes (preferably Roma,
outdoor- and vine-ripened) or 2 x 400 g
cans of peeled chopped tomatoes in juice
3 tablespoons tomato purée
1 teaspoon fresh chopped oregano
salt and freshly ground black pepper

For the parmigiana
4 large red capsicums
olive oil spray
3 large aubergines
2 cups grated tasty cheese
½ cup finely grated Parmesan
freshly ground black pepper

To make the sauce, melt the butter and olive oil in a large saucepan. Add the onions and garlic and cook for 2–3 minutes. Blanch the tomatoes and remove skins. Roughly chop the tomatoes and add, with the tomato purée and oregano, to the onions and garlic. Simmer uncovered for 25–30 minutes, stirring often, until the sauce is thick and pulpy. Season as desired.

To prepare the parmigiana, quarter, core and deseed the capsicums. Spray the skin sides with oil and grill or place on barbecue for 5–6 minutes until the skin chars. Place in a plastic bag, seal and cool. When cool, rub the skins off.

Cut the aubergines lengthways into thick slices. Spray with oil then grill or barbecue for 6–8 minutes each side. Set aside to cool.

Preheat the oven to 200°C. Spray a 20 cm x 30 cm lasagne dish with baking spray. Spoon a quarter of the tomato sauce into the base of the dish. Layer the capsicum and aubergine slices, alternating with cheese, tomato sauce and lots of black pepper. Finish with Parmesan and another grind of pepper. Bake for 35–40 minutes until golden brown. Serve with a green salad and crusty bread.

If you are pushed for time, you can use canned tomato purée or store-bought pasta sauce. For a dinner party, I recommend making your own rich tomato sauce.

Hoisin Pork Wraps

Serves 4

1 tablespoon canola or lite olive oil
2 teaspoons sesame oil
1 tablespoon grated fresh ginger
700 g pork fillet, finely sliced
½ cup hoisin sauce
4 large flour tortillas
½ cucumber, grated
5 spring onions, finely sliced
bunch watercress leaves

Heat oils in a large non-stick frypan. Add the ginger and pork slices and stir-fry for 3–4 minutes until the pork loses its pinkness. Add the hoisin sauce and cook for a further minute in the pan. Warm the tortillas. (I find it best to wrap them in paper towels and heat them in the microwave.)

Spread each warmed tortilla with one-quarter of the pork and sauce. Top with grated cucumber, spring onions and watercress. Roll up snugly and cut in half. Eat immediately.

Oven-baked Bacon, Pea and Parmesan Risotto

If you're a purist, you won't approve of my short-cut oven-baked risotto, but I think adding all the stock in one go makes very little difference to the final dish and saves a huge amount of tiddling about. This is a very useful recipe when time and energy are in short supply.

Serves 4–6

3 tablespoons olive oil
50 g butter
2 onions, finely chopped
1–2 cloves garlic, crushed (1 teaspoon)
8 rashers rindless bacon, chopped
1½ cups Arborio (risotto) rice
4½ cups good chicken stock
1 cup frozen baby peas
1 cup finely grated Parmesan
extra knob of butter (optional)
salt and freshly ground black pepper

Preheat the oven to 180°C.

Heat the olive oil and butter in a large ovenproof pan. Add the onion and fry for 5 minutes to soften but not brown. Add the garlic and cook for a further minute, then add the bacon. Cook this for a couple of minutes then add the rice and stock. Mix well and cover with a tight-fitting lid or tinfoil. Bake for 35–40 minutes.

By this time most of the stock will have been absorbed. Stir through the peas and Parmesan and the extra knob of butter, if using. Season as desired and serve immediately.

Ginger, Sweet Chilli and Coconut Cream Chicken

Serve this tasty chicken with jasmine rice and bok choy.

Serves 4

2 tablespoons oil
4 large skinless and boneless chicken breasts, sliced
2–3 cloves garlic, crushed (1 teaspoon)
1 tablespoon grated fresh ginger
1 small onion or 2 shallots, finely chopped
1 red capsicum, deseeded and chopped
grated rind and juice of 1 lemon
1 x 200 g can sliced bamboo shoots, drained
1 x 400 g can coconut cream
200 ml sweet chilli sauce
5 spring onions, sliced
½ cup chopped coriander leaves or parsley,
plus extra coriander to garnish

Heat the oil in a large non-stick frypan and fry the sliced chicken for 6–7 minutes. Add the garlic, ginger, onion and capsicum and fry together for a further 2 minutes. Once the onion has softened, add the lemon rind and juice, bamboo shoots, coconut cream and sweet chilli sauce. Turn the heat down to a simmer and cook for 3–4 minutes. Add the spring onions and coriander, stir through and garnish with a little extra coriander.

Cook School Tips for Using Chopsticks

- *It is considered rude to point chopsticks at people.*
- *Chopsticks pointing upwards are believed to bring bad luck. Lie them flat across the top of your bowl or plate with tips pointing left.*

*Clever ingredients with a
little handling produce
big results.*

Peppercorn Steaks with Jack Daniel's Gravy

These are great with broccoli or green beans and baked potatoes
in their jackets.

Serves 6

―⁂―

For the steaks

4 teaspoons coarsely crushed black peppercorns
½ teaspoon salt flakes
6 x fillet steaks, 180–250 g each
1 tablespoon oil (canola or ricebran)

For the gravy

100 g butter, cut into small pieces
½ cup chopped shallots or finely chopped onion
¾ cup beef stock
¾ cup Jack Daniel's (or bourbon)
½ teaspoon Worcestershire sauce

To prepare the steaks, mix the crushed peppercorns and salt together on a plate.
Brush the steaks all over with oil, then sprinkle with the pepper mixture, pressing
firmly to adhere. Heat a large, heavy frypan over medium to high heat and add
the steaks, cooking for 3 minutes on each side for medium rare. Remove from
pan and rest on a warm plate, covered in tinfoil, while you prepare the gravy.

To make the gravy, melt a few cubes of butter in the steak pan and add the
shallots, frying for 2–3 minutes until softened and starting to brown. Add the
stock and spirits and simmer for 3–4 minutes to reduce the volume by half. Whisk
in the remainder of the butter and the Worcestershire sauce. Spoon over the steaks
and serve immediately.

Chicken Burgers with Asian Slaw

The slaw will serve 6 as a side dish.

Makes 8 burgers

—∿∿—

For the slaw
6 cups finely shredded Chinese
cabbage (½–1 cabbage)
3 spring onions, finely sliced
½ telegraph cucumber, finely sliced
3 stalks celery, finely sliced
½ red capsicum, deseeded and
very finely sliced
1 handful fresh coriander leaves,
chopped
½ cup chopped parsley
1 cup bean sprouts

For the slaw dressing
¼ cup sweet chilli sauce
¼ cup rice wine vinegar
grated rind and juice of 3–4 limes
¾ cup extra-virgin olive oil
1 tablespoon sesame oil
1 teaspoon crushed or finely chopped
fresh ginger

For the burgers
750 g skinless and boneless chicken
meat (thigh or breast)
½ cup hoisin sauce
1–2 teaspoons chilli paste
1–2 cloves garlic, crushed (½ teaspoon)
1 handful coriander leaves, chopped
1 teaspoon finely chopped or
grated fresh ginger
8 sesame rolls

To make the slaw, place all the salad ingredients in a large bowl.

To make the dressing, place all the ingredients in a screw-top jar and shake to
combine. Drizzle over the salad and toss vigorously to mix the dressing through.

To make the burger patties, place all ingredients except the sesame rolls in
a food processor and run the machine to finely chop the meat and mix all the
ingredients together. Form into 8 burger patties and pan fry for 3–4 minutes on
each side to cook through. Serve in soft sesame bread rolls with Asian slaw and,
if desired, extra sweet chilli sauce.

Dukkah-coated Fish Fillets

You can easily buy dukkah but there is something quite special about making your own.

Serves 4

For the dukkah (makes 4 cups)
1 cup sesame seeds
3 tablespoons whole coriander seeds
2 tablespoons whole cumin seeds
½ cup pine nuts
1 cup peeled and chopped hazelnuts
1½ cups coarsely chopped almonds
1 tablespoon salt
1 teaspoon coarsely ground black pepper

For the fish
4 fish fillets (snapper, blue cod, etc)
½ cup olive oil
2–3 cloves garlic, crushed (1 teaspoon)
¼ cup white wine vinegar
1 teaspoon ground cumin
¾ cup dukkah

To make the dukkah, place all the ingredients in a large non-stick frypan over medium heat and dry fry for 4–5 minutes, stirring continuously until the aroma starts to be released. No need to add any oil or fat! Cool the mixture, then place in a food processor and run the machine until coarsely chopped. You may need to do the processing in batches. Dukkah will keep in an airtight jar in the pantry for up to 6 weeks.

To prepare the fish, preheat the oven to 180°C. Rinse the fish fillets and pat dry with paper towels. Whisk the olive oil, garlic, vinegar and cumin together and pour over the fish. Marinate in the fridge for 15–20 minutes — any longer and the fish will soften too much and become quite mushy.

Place the dukkah on a plate, ready to coat the fish. Drain the fish and press down into the dukkah to coat well on both sides. Place fish in a roasting dish and bake for 15–20 minutes until the fish is cooked through. Serve with crisp green salad, French fries and lemon wedges.

Maple and Lime Roasted Salmon with Fresh Asparagus

Serves 6

For the marinade

6 portions skinned and boned salmon fillet
(I use portions about the size of a Weet-Bix)
grated rind and juice of 3 limes
2 tablespoons pure maple syrup (or honey)

For the asparagus

2 large handfuls thin asparagus (about 48 spears), sliced into four
1 tablespoon marinade

Preheat the oven to 200°C. To prepare the marinade, place salmon portions in a roasting dish. Mix the lime rind and juice with the maple syrup. Drizzle the marinade over the salmon, reserving 1 tablespoon of the mixture. Roast for 12 minutes.

While the salmon is cooking, prepare the asparagus. Bring a saucepan of salted water to the boil and add the trimmed, sliced asparagus. Cook for 2 minutes then drain and toss with the reserved marinade.

Spoon onto 6 warmed serving plates and top each pile of asparagus with a salmon portion. Serve with a crisp green salad and rice or mashed potatoes.

Persian Lamb-stuffed Pita Breads with Minted Yoghurt Sauce

This dinner is easy to make in a microwave and is big on flavour.

Serves 6

For the minted yoghurt sauce
1 cup thick natural yoghurt
2 tablespoons mint jelly or thick mint sauce
2 tablespoons chopped parsley
1 tablespoon chopped mint

For the pita pockets
6 pita breads
500 g minced lamb
2 teaspoons mild curry powder
1 packet leek and potato soup mix (powder)
½ cup sultanas
½ cup long-thread coconut
¼ cup sliced almonds
2 cups thick natural yoghurt
3 tablespoons chopped parsley
shredded lettuce to serve

To make the sauce, mix all ingredients together and keep covered in the fridge.

To heat the pita breads, wrap in paper towels and warm in the microwave, or wrap in tinfoil and warm in the oven.

To prepare the mince, put it in a large microwaveproof bowl and sprinkle with the curry powder and soup powder. Microwave on high in bursts of 1 minute for about 5–6 minutes, stirring after each burst, until no pinkness remains in the meat. Add the sultanas, coconut and almonds. Mix well and cook for 1 minute more. Stir through the yoghurt and parsley. Open the pita breads and fill with the mixture and shredded lettuce. Serve with minted yoghurt sauce.

Start your own culinary traditions. You don't need to have grown up in the Walton family to enjoy Sunday lunch together.

Red Wine Risotto with Radicchio and Blue Cheese

Serves 4

2 tablespoons olive oil
1 large red onion, finely chopped
6 rashers rindless bacon, chopped
1 x 750 ml bottle light red wine (pinot noir is ideal)
1 litre vegetable or chicken stock
300 g Arborio rice
½ teaspoon salt
2 small radicchio, sliced
50 g butter
150 g blue cheese, crumbled
¼ cup cream
2 tablespoons chopped flat-leafed parsley to garnish

Heat the oil in a large non-stick frypan, add the onion and cook over medium heat for a few minutes. Add the bacon. In a separate saucepan, bring the red wine and stock to the boil then reduce heat to just simmering. Add the rice to the onion mixture and stir to heat through and coat each rice grain. Add the wine and stock a ladle at a time to the rice and stir continuously as the liquid is absorbed. The stirring action releases the starch in the rice, which gives the risotto its lovely creamy texture. When the rice is softened but not overcooked, add the salt to taste, radicchio and butter. Stir as the radicchio wilts.

Place the blue cheese and cream in a small saucepan and gently melt together. Serve the risotto in pasta bowls with the blue cheese cream poured over and a good sprinkling of chopped parsley.

Southern Beer-braised Lamb Shanks

Southern as in 'Southern Man' — from the lower part of New Zealand's
South Island, which is famous for Speight's beer.

Serves 4

For the shanks
4 large lamb shanks
salt and freshly ground black pepper
1 tablespoon flour
1 tablespoon oil
4 slices rindless bacon, chopped
1 large onion, roughly chopped
2 carrots, roughly chopped
1 small bunch thyme sprigs
2–3 cloves garlic, crushed (1 teaspoon)
1 tablespoon brown sugar
1½ cups brown lentils
2 cups well-flavoured beef or lamb stock
1 x 330 ml bottle Speight's beer
grated rind and juice of 1 lemon

For the garnish
grated lemon rind
thyme sprigs
1 tablespoon chopped
flat-leafed parsley

Preheat the oven to 180°C.

Sprinkle the shanks with salt and black pepper and dust with flour. Heat the
oil in a large ovenproof frypan or casserole dish. Brown the shanks and cook
for 5–6 minutes, turning to brown evenly. Remove shanks to a plate. Fry the
bacon for 2–3 minutes then add the onion, carrots, thyme and garlic. Cook
for 2 minutes before stirring in the brown sugar, lentils, stock, beer and lemon
rind and juice. Add the shanks, cover with a lid or tinfoil and cook in the oven
for 1½ hours, until the meat is tender and falling off the bones. Check halfway
through cooking and turn the shanks to cook evenly. Garnish with lemon rind,
thyme sprigs and chopped parsley and serve with mashed potatoes.

Cook School Tips for Making Gravy

If you know how to make a roast, you can also learn how to make good gravy. The following guidelines will give you 2 cups of gravy — enough to serve 4–6 people.

1 Remove the roasted meat from the roasting dish and transfer to a plate, covering with tinfoil to keep warm.

2 Pour the meat juices into a jug, add ice cubes and allow the fat to solidify. Return 2 tablespoons of the fat back into the roasting dish and discard the rest of the fat.

3 Place the dish over medium heat. Add 2 tablespoons of flour and, scraping the bottom of the dish with a silicone spatula, cook for 2–3 minutes.

4 Make the jug of pan juices up to 2 cups with either stock or water.

5 Stir the juice mixture into the roasting dish and simmer for 3–4 minutes until thickened.

6 For extra flavour you can add port, herbs or fruit paste.

Slow cooking is good
because time, not fat, creates
the flavour.

Greek Lamb Cutlets with Avgolemono Sauce

Serves 6

For the cutlets

18 lamb cutlets, cut French style
(with long trimmed bones)
salt and freshly ground black pepper
6 slices white toast-cut bread,
crusts removed
2–3 cloves garlic, crushed (1 teaspoon)
1 small handful mint leaves,
plus extra to garnish
grated rind of 2 lemons
100 g feta cheese, crumbled
¼ cup extra-virgin olive oil
12 vine-ripened small or cherry
tomatoes with stems attached

For the sauce

2 tablespoons cold water
1 teaspoon cornflour
4 egg yolks
grated rind and juice of 2 large lemons
300 ml well-flavoured
chicken stock, hot
5 spring onions, finely sliced

Preheat the oven to 200°C. To prepare the cutlets, season on both sides and bash the meaty pieces flat with a steak hammer. Place the bread in a food processor and process to form crumbs. Add the garlic, mint, lemon rind, feta and 1 tablespoon of oil. Pulse until just combined. Heat the remaining oil in a large ovenproof frypan. Add the cutlets and fry for 1 minute on each side. Place a small amount of the crumb mixture on top of each cutlet (transfer to a roasting dish if the pan doesn't hold them all). Cook in the oven for 5–6 minutes, then add the whole tomatoes and cook for a further 2 minutes. The crumbs should be golden brown and the tomatoes still intact.

While the lamb is in the oven, make the sauce by mixing the cold water and cornflour together to form a smooth paste. Whisk the egg yolks, lemon rind and juice in a small saucepan. Add the cornflour paste. Add 2 tablespoons of the hot stock, whisking well. Pour in the remaining stock and spring onions. Stir over gentle heat. Do not boil, but keep stirring as it thickens. To serve, pour sauce over the cutlets and garnish with mint. (The sauce tends to split if reheated.)

This classic Greek egg and lemon sauce is perfect with roast lamb or hogget. It moisturises like gravy, but with a *fresh citrus attitude*.

Scallop Rice Cakes with Coriander and Lime Mayonnaise

Serves 4

For the rice cakes

3 cups cooked rice

12 scallops, each cut into 4–5 pieces

2 teaspoons minced fresh ginger

¼ cup chopped parsley

¼ cup chopped coriander leaves

4 eggs

½ teaspoon salt

½ teaspoon freshly ground black pepper

1 teaspoon Asian fish sauce

¼ cup oil

sweet chilli sauce to serve

For the mayonnaise

1 cup homemade or good-quality store-bought mayonnaise

grated rind and juice of 2 limes

½ cup chopped coriander leaves

To make the rice cakes, mix all ingredients together except the oil and sweet chilli sauce. Heat the oil in a large non-stick frypan. Form half-cups of mixture into cake shapes and fry four cakes at a time for 2–3 minutes on each side until golden. Drain on paper towels and keep warm while you cook the remainder of the mixture.

To make the mayonnaise, mix all ingredients together. Serve the warm rice cakes with dollops of coriander lime mayonnaise and sweet chilli sauce on the side.

Linguine with Prawns, Asparagus and Sauvignon Blanc Butter Sauce

The few simple ingredients are tossed together to produce a rich pasta dish
that's perfect for entertaining.

Serves 6

500 g linguine pasta
50 g butter
1 large onion, finely chopped
300 ml sauvignon blanc
500 ml lite crème fraîche
salt and freshly ground black pepper
350 g thin asparagus spears, chopped
500 g cooked and shelled prawns
1 bunch dill, chopped (about 3 tablespoons)

Cook the pasta in a large saucepan of generously salted boiling water until tender.

Melt the butter in a large frypan, add the onion and gently cook to soften it without browning. Add the wine and bring to the boil, reducing the liquid by half. Add the crème fraîche and season as desired.

Cook the asparagus in boiling water for 2–3 minutes until just tender. Drain and add to the sauce with the prawns and dill. Drain the pasta and add to the sauce, tossing well to mix everything together. Serve immediately.

Home

Home is where your memories
are stored.

Fish Fillets Baked with Chorizo and Cannellini Beans

A crisp green leafy salad is the perfect accompaniment for this rustic dish.

Serves 4

2 tablespoons olive oil
5 spring onions, sliced
1 medium red capsicum, deseeded and chopped
100 g (approximately 3) chorizo sausages, sliced
2 x 400 g cans cannellini beans, drained and rinsed
4 tablespoons chopped flat-leafed parsley
salt and freshly ground black pepper
300 ml vegetable or chicken stock
4 x 100 g skinless and boneless fish fillets (snapper, terakihi or cod)
parsley to garnish

Preheat the oven to 180°C. Heat the oil in an ovenproof frypan. Fry the spring onions and chopped capsicum for 3–4 minutes. Add the chorizo, beans and parsley. Mix well and season as desired. Add the stock and place the fish on top. Bake for 12–15 minutes until the fish is opaque and just cooked though. You can leave the fillets whole, cut into bite-sized chunks or flake the fish into chunky pieces with a fork before stirring through the beans. Serve immediately with a smattering of parsley on top.

Warm Lamb, Feta and Pasta Salad

This can be served warm or cold and is perfect for a smart picnic. It can be
made up to 3 days ahead and stored in the fridge.

Serves 4

300 g dried spiral pasta
1 teaspoon olive oil
600 g lamb fillets or shortloins, trimmed of all
silver skin and sliced into bite-sized chunks
½ cup olive oil
1 cup chopped parsley
10–12 mint leaves, chopped
10–12 basil leaves, chopped
1 tablespoon grainy mustard
2 tablespoons capers, drained
grated rind and juice of 2 lemons
1 red capsicum, deseeded and sliced
1 punnet cherry tomatoes, halved
1 cup crumbled or cubed feta
1 cup black olives
salt and freshly ground black pepper

Cook the pasta in a large saucepan of generously salted boiling water until
tender. Meanwhile, heat a large non-stick frypan with the first measure of oil
and pan fry the lamb for about 3 minutes until just cooked, but still pink.
Remove to a plate and cover with tinfoil, leaving it to rest for 5 minutes.

Toss all other ingredients except seasoning in a large bowl. Add the drained
pasta and lamb slices, plus any juices that have accumulated. Season as desired
and serve immediately or cover and store in the fridge until required.

Tagliatelle with Hazelnut Parsley Pesto and Baby Rocket

Simple preparation and fabulous flavours — need I say more?

Serves 4

For the pesto

1 cup chopped flat-leafed parsley
1 cup toasted hazelnuts, skins rubbed off
1 cup grated Parmesan, plus extra to garnish
grated rind and juice of 1 lemon
100 ml extra-virgin olive oil
salt and freshly ground black pepper

For the tagliatelle

400 g tagliatelle, fettuccine or spaghetti
2 handfuls baby rocket leaves

To make the pesto, place the parsley, hazelnuts, Parmesan and lemon rind and juice in a food processor. Whiz together as you slowly drizzle in the olive oil. Season as desired.

Cook the pasta in a large saucepan of generously salted boiling water until tender. Drain the pasta and mix in the pesto and rocket leaves, tossing to combine well. Add extra Parmesan to garnish.

Pappardelle with Anchovies and Raisins

This is a classic Sicilian summer dish that is quick and easy to prepare, but will always gets rave reviews. Leave out the anchovies for a vegetarian version, but without them you will probably have to season the dish with salt.

Serves 4

400–500 g pappardelle (broad flat ribbon pasta)
1 head broccoli, broken into florets (stems peeled, if desired)
4 tablespoons olive oil (or 1–2 tablespoons of oil
from the anchovies made up to 4 tablespoons with olive oil)
1 large red onion, sliced
2–3 cloves garlic, crushed (1 teaspoon)
½ cup pine nuts, toasted (can be done in a microwave)
½ cup raisins
1 x 50 g can anchovies in oil, drained and chopped
½ cup chopped flat-leafed parsley
freshly ground black pepper

Cook the pasta in a large saucepan of generously salted boiling water until tender.

Just before the pasta is cooked, toss in the prepared broccoli and cook until just tender (only a few minutes). Drain in a colander. Add oil to the hot saucepan and cook the onion and garlic for a couple of minutes to soften. Return the pasta to the pan and toss with the toasted pine nuts, raisins, anchovies and parsley. Season with pepper and serve immediately.

Orecchiette filled with Parmesan, Basil and Pine Nuts

Orecchiotte are giant ear-shaped pasta shells suitable for filling. Orecchiette
are a smaller version, usually served with sauce. They can be bought
from smart supermarkets and good delis.

Serves 4

12 orecchiette
2 tablespoons basil pesto
125 g cream cheese
½ cup grated Parmesan
¼ cup pine nuts
salt and freshly ground black pepper
1 x 500 g jar store-bought tomato-based pasta sauce
1 x 400 g can chopped tomatoes in juice
fresh basil leaves to garnish

Bring a large saucepan of generously salted water to the boil and, using a slotted
spoon, carefully lower the orecchiette in. Keep the water gently boiling and cook
the pasta for 15–18 minutes. Do not allow the water to boil vigorously as this
may damage the pasta. Carefully lift out the pasta and cool on the bench.

Preheat the oven to 160°C. Mix the pesto, cream cheese, Parmesan and pine
nuts together and season as desired. Fill the pasta ears with the cheese mixture
using a gentle hand.

Mix the pasta sauce with the tomatoes in juice and pour into the bottom of
an ovenproof lasagne or gratin dish. Carefully nestle the filled orecchiette into
the tomato mixture and cover with a tight-fitting lid or tinfoil. Bake for 25–30
minutes. Serve individual portions with a little pool of sauce and the pasta
sitting on top. Garnish with basil leaves.

Baked Ricotta and Tomato Tortellini

Serves 6

250 g ricotta cheese (1 tub)
2–3 cloves garlic, crushed (1 teaspoon)
1 cup fresh basil leaves, loosely packed
2 x 400 g packets fresh tortellini
(I like beef and sundried tomato tortellini)
3 x 400 g cans chopped tomatoes in juice
1 punnet cherry tomatoes
salt and freshly ground black pepper
1 cup grated mozzarella

Preheat the oven to 200°C. Spray a 20 cm x 30 cm lasagne dish with baking spray.

Place the ricotta, garlic and most of the basil, reserving a few small leaves for garnishing, in a food processor and mix really well.

Cook the pasta in a large saucepan of generously salted boiling water for 3 minutes until partially cooked. Drain the pasta and tip it into the prepared dish. Pour the chopped tomatoes and juice into the dish and mix through the pasta. Sprinkle the basil ricotta mixture evenly over the pasta and dot with cherry tomatoes. Generously season with salt and black pepper. Sprinkle with mozzarella and bake, uncovered, for 20–25 minutes until bubbling around the edges and the cheese is melted and browning. Sprinkle with the reserved basil leaves to garnish.

5. Bits on the Side

Real nutrition is about eating foods
that are full of flavour and in season
that bring you pleasure and feed
your soul, too. This is where side
dishes come into their own.

Lebanese Couscous and Orzo

Lebanese couscous is made from durum wheat flour and is a lot larger
than regular couscous. Because of its size it needs to be boiled.
It is a fine alternative to rice, pasta or mashed potatoes.

Serves 6

1½ cups Lebanese couscous
1½ cups orzo pasta
2 teaspoons salt
50 g butter or 2 tablespoons olive oil
freshly ground black pepper
1 cup chopped parsley

Bring a large saucepan of water to the boil. Add the couscous and orzo with the
salt. Boil for 5 minutes, stirring a couple of times. Turn off heat and rest for at
least 10 minutes. Drain, after checking the couscous and orzo are tender to the
bite. Stir in the butter or oil, pepper and parsley.

Soft, Creamy Polenta

This is another fine alternative to rice, pasta, mashed potatoes or couscous.

Serves 6

1 teaspoon salt
2 cups milk
4 cups well-flavoured chicken stock
1½ cups polenta (not the instant variety)
½ teaspoon freshly ground black pepper
¾ cup finely grated Parmesan
knob of butter, if desired

Bring salt, milk and stock to the boil in a large saucepan. Whisking slowly, pour the polenta into the saucepan and continue whisking to prevent lumps forming. Reduce heat to the gentlest simmer and stir often as the polenta bubbles away for about 15–20 minutes, until creamy and soft. Add the pepper, Parmesan and butter, if using. Serve immediately.

Cook School Tips for Perfect Mashed Potatoes

To make the perfect mashed potatoes you need to begin with the right sort of spud. There is no such thing as an all-purpose spud. You need a good mashing variety, such as my favourite Agria potatoes.

- Peel the potatoes before you cook them. While its good to keep the skin on when you can, it doesn't look great in the mash, and stops it becoming light and fluffy.

- Boil the potatoes until tender when pricked with a knife. Drain all the water from the potatoes before mashing.

- Use a potato ricer to increase the fluffiness of the potatoes. A masher can often turn the whole mixture into thick glue.

- Warm the milk before you add it to the mash. Cold milk can turn the potato starch into gluey paste, instead of keeping it light and fluffy.

- Make up a huge batch of mashed potato and freeze it. Take it out in the morning and it will be ready to heat by dinnertime.

- If you are cooking for a crowd and want to prepare mashed potatoes early in the day, make the batch then lay a piece of paper on the top to stop it from drying out. Warm in the oven or microwave.

Garlic and Feta Spinach Mash

I like to use Agria potatoes for this flash mash.

Serves 4–6

---

1 kg mashing potatoes, peeled and cut into 2 cm cubes
¾ cup milk (or cream if you're allowed)
4–5 cloves garlic, crushed (2 teaspoons)
50 g butter
500 g frozen spinach, thawed and squeezed to remove
excess liquid (do this in a sieve)
100 g feta, crumbled
salt and finely ground white pepper

Boil the potatoes until tender then press through a potato ricer, or mash
thoroughly. Heat the milk or cream with the garlic in the saucepan the potatoes
were cooked in. Add the butter and spinach to warm through. Mix in the
mashed potato and stir the feta through. Season carefully, remembering that feta
is quite salty.

Hash Browns

Hash browns go with just about anything, but I especially enjoy them with a
fresh and spicy peach salsa (see page 262).

Serves 4

4 large red-skinned potatoes, scrubbed
salt and freshly ground black pepper
3 tablespoons oil
25 g butter

Bring the potatoes to the boil and boil for 5 minutes before turning off the
heat and leaving them to go cold in the water. (Potatoes can be cooked a day
in advance.) When cool, grate the potatoes, skin and all. (I do this in a food
processor fitted with a grating disc.) The potatoes should be firm and too raw to
eat. Season the grated potato generously with salt and black pepper.

Heat a large non-stick frypan over medium to high heat. Add the oil and
butter. When the butter is melted and sizzling, add the grated potato mix in
four equal piles. Flatten each pile slightly with a fish slice and cook until golden,
crispy and brown. Turn over and cook the other side. Drain on paper towels and
serve warm.

Squashed New Season Potatoes with Lemon and Fresh Bay Leaves

Serves 6

30–36 small new season potatoes (I use Jersey Bennes)
6–12 fresh bay leaves
grated rind and juice of 2 lemons
¼ cup extra-virgin olive oil
salt and freshly ground black pepper

Scrub the potatoes and boil them in their skins for 8–10 minutes until just cooked. Drain and cool so that they are easily handled without burning your fingers.

Preheat the oven to 200°C. Spray a roasting dish with baking spray. Spread the bay leaves in the base of the pan then squash the little potatoes into the leaves. Press them down until the skin splits and they squish open — don't mash them.

Whisk together the lemon rind and juice and the oil. Drizzle over the potatoes then generously sprinkle with salt and black pepper. Roast for 30–40 minutes until crispy and golden brown.

*Always show **hospitality** to strangers. Unwittingly, you may be entertaining an angel.*

*Cook School Tips
for Perfect Poached Eggs*

This is a cunning method for a quick poached egg with minimum fuss
and a quick clean-up.

1 Crack the egg into a small noodle bowl or cup lined with cling film with a
sizable overhang, or a tiny snack-size plastic ziplock bag.

2 Pull up the corners of the cling film, twisting and knotting the top to enclose
the egg as tightly as possible without leaving too much of an air pocket.

3 Boil water in a small saucepan or electric kettle. Turn off heat and lower the
egg in for 4 minutes.

4 Snip the top knot off the cling film or cut open the ziplock bag and, hey
presto — a perfect, firm but gooey-in-the-centre poached egg.

5 Place the egg onto toast, a toasted bagel or Squashed New Season Potatoes
with Lemon and Fresh Bay Leaves (see page 225) and pass the hollandaise!

Peas with Lemon, Chives and Artichokes

This lovely vegetable dish is equally delicious served
hot as a side dish or cold as a salad.

Serves 4

---

3 cups frozen baby peas (unminted), thawed
1 x 400 g can artichoke hearts in brine, drained and chopped
grated rind and juice of 2 lemons
2 tablespoons chopped chives
2 tablespoons extra-virgin olive oil
salt and freshly ground black pepper

Heat a saucepan of salted water to boiling. Add the peas and boil for 2 minutes,
then add the chopped artichokes just for 30 seconds to warm. Drain and toss
with the lemon rind and juice, chives and olive oil. Season as desired.

Serve warm or at room temperature. Store covered in the fridge if not eating
straight away.

Roasted Radishes

This very simple and tasty treat comes from an easily grown vegetable that, often as not, produces a summer glut. The radishes' hot flavour caramelises and becomes very mellow — they're quite different from raw radishes. In the café we use a variety called Easter Egg — it's a large, round radish that is delicious prepared this way.

———

Preheat the oven to 180°C or heat a barbecue plate. Scrub and top and tail the radishes and coat well with oil. (I usually pour the oil into my hands and rub the radishes.) Salt generously and either cook in a roasting tin in the oven or on the barbecue for 20–30 minutes until cooked through. They should be soft when pierced with a knife. Serve in a large bowl as you would new potatoes.

Green Beans with Toasted Sesame Dressing

This can be served as a hot side dish or cold salad and is a perfect accompaniment to Asian-style main courses.

Serves 6

For the dressing
3 tablespoons sesame seeds
2 spring onions, finely sliced
1–2 cloves garlic, crushed (½ teaspoon)
1 tablespoon light soy sauce
2 teaspoons sesame oil
1 teaspoon liquid honey
1 teaspoon grated fresh ginger

For the beans
500 g small green beans (2 handfuls)

To make the dressing, toast the sesame seeds in a dry non-stick frypan, stirring over medium heat for 5–6 minutes as they turn a golden nutty brown. Alternatively, dry toast them in a microwave for bursts of 10 seconds on high, stirring between each burst as the seeds brown in the centre first. Mix the hot seeds with the spring onion, garlic, soy, sesame oil, honey and ginger.

To prepare the beans, bring a saucepan of water to the boil and cook the beans for 3–4 minutes. Drain in a colander, place in a serving bowl and toss in the dressing.

The dressing can be made ahead of time and the beans cooked then plunged into cold water to preserve their fresh green colour. They can be reheated in the microwave just before serving.

Jacket Spuds with Smoked Fish and Cheesy Crumbs

Jacket potatoes can be stuffed with whatever you fancy, but his particular combination is my all-time favourite comfort food for a rainy-day supper.

Serves 4

4 large baking potatoes, scrubbed
1 tablespoon olive oil
500 g smoked fish fillets
2 tablespoons crème fraîche or cream cheese
1 large handful grated tasty cheese
50 g butter
1 tablespoon snipped chives or finely sliced spring onion
1 egg
½ cup frozen baby peas

Preheat the oven to 200°C. Rub the scrubbed potatoes with the oil and prick with a small knife. Bake for an hour until completely tender and the skins crispy.

Flake the fish off the skin and remove any bones. You can soften the fish in boiling water if it seems a bit dry.

When the potatoes are cool enough to handle, cut a thin slice off each one and, leaving a decent border so that it will hold its shape, scoop out the potato flesh into a bowl. Mash the potato flesh with the crème fraîche, grated cheese, butter, chives and egg. When well mixed, fold in the peas and smoked fish. Divide the mixture evenly between the potato shells.

Place in a small roasting dish and bake for 20 minutes until warmed through and tinged nice and golden brown. As soon as they have cooled enough to eat, tuck in!

Roasted Pear and Blue Cheese Salad with Honey and Mint Dressing

Serves 6

For the salad

3 pears, cored and quartered

1 tablespoon olive oil

3 handfuls salad greens (mesclun, baby spinach, etc)

150 g soft blue cheese (I use Blue Castello), crumbled into pieces

½ cup fresh walnut halves

½ cup chopped parsley

For the dressing

2 tablespoons liquid honey

1 handful mint leaves (about 1 cup)

½ teaspoon salt

freshly ground black pepper

2 tablespoons white wine vinegar

1 tablespoon Dijon mustard

2 cups soya or canola oil

Preheat the oven to 200°C.

To prepare the pears, drizzle the pear quarters with olive oil and roast in the oven for 15–20 minutes, until softened and starting to colour.

Arrange salad greens on plates and place roasted pear quarters on the greens. Divide the blue cheese and walnuts between the salad portions.

To prepare the dressing, place all ingredients in a blender and process until well combined.

Drizzle the salad with the honey and mint dressing and sprinkle with parsley.

Warm Summer Garden Salad

This salad is definitely about seasonal vegetables. There is no strict
ingredient list — it all depends on what is available on the day
at the market or from your garden.

Serves 6

For the salad
5–6 cups prepared fresh vegetables
2 handfuls salad leaves
½ cup summer herbs, roughly torn or chopped

For the dressing
grated rind and juice of 1 orange
1 teaspoon liquid honey
1 teaspoon Dijon mustard
2 tablespoons white wine vinegar
¼ cup extra-virgin olive or avocado oil
salt and freshly ground black pepper

Fill a large saucepan with water and bring it to the boil.

Meanwhile, wash the salad leaves and herbs and dry off in a salad spinner
or shake in a tea towel. Whisk the dressing ingredients together and place in a
squeezy bottle or small jug.

Cook the vegetables very lightly in the boiling water, starting with the hard
vegetables such as carrots as they will take longer to cook. Drain the vegetables
in a colander then place in a serving dish. Add the dressing and toss. Just before
serving, add the salad leaves and herbs. Serve immediately as the leafy greens
start wilting in the warmth of the cooked vegetables.

Remember the day's blessings.
Forget the day's troubles.

Chickpea and Roasted Pumpkin Salad

Serves 4–6

½ cup olive oil
1.5 kg butternut pumpkin, peeled, deseeded and cut into small cubes
1 x 400 g can chickpeas, drained and rinsed
½ cup roasted red capsicum in brine or oil, drained
½ small red onion, finely chopped
1 cup chopped flat-leafed parsley
5 spring onions, finely sliced
grated rind and juice of 2 lemons
1 teaspoon mixed spice
½ teaspoon mild curry powder
5 pieces crystallised ginger, chopped
4–5 dried figs, chopped
2 tablespoons olive oil

Preheat the oven to 200°C.

Place the first measure of olive oil and the pumpkin in a roasting dish. Stir to coat well and roast for 20 minutes until the pumpkin is just tender. Add the warm pumpkin to the other ingredients, tossing well to really mix together. Serve at room temperature.

Quinoa — pronounced keen-wah — is **an ancient grain from Peru.** *It is higher in protein and lower in carbohydrates than many other grains and* **can be used instead of rice** *in many recipes. This salad is best made 2–3 hours ahead of time to allow the flavours to develop.*

Thai Basil and Quinoa Salad

Makes 8 cups — enough to serve 8 as a side salad

For the salad
2 cups quinoa
1 teaspoon salt
1 cup deseeded and finely chopped tomato
1 cup chopped flat-leafed parsley
1 cup peeled, deseeded and finely chopped cucumber
5 spring onions, finely sliced

For the dressing
½ cup extra-virgin olive oil
grated rind and juice of 3 lemons
½ teaspoon ground cumin
½ teaspoon ground cinnamon
½ cup chopped Thai basil or fresh mint
salt and freshly ground black pepper

To make the salad, rinse the quinoa in a sieve under cold running water. Place in a saucepan with salt and 5 cups of water. Bring to the boil, stirring a couple of times. Place the lid on the saucepan and reduce heat to a very low simmer for 15 minutes. (The liquid should be absorbed and the grain translucent and chewy but tender.) Cool the quinoa then mix with the other salad ingredients.

To make the dressing, put all the ingredients in a screw-top jar and shake to combine. Drizzle over the salad and toss to mix the dressing through.

Store covered in the fridge until required.

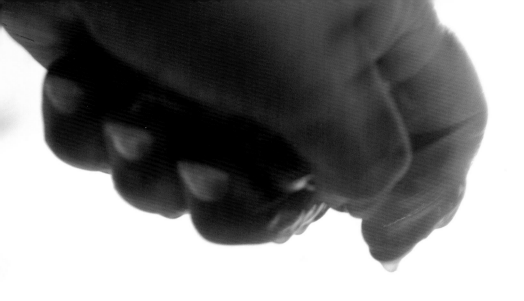

This is a ***fire and ice*** kind of salad — fiery
from the chilli yet cool as a cucumber. It's
***delicious with simple barbecued or
grilled chicken or fish.***

Spicy Cucumber and Chilli Salad

Serves 4

1 large telegraph cucumber, peeled
2 teaspoons sweet chilli sauce
1 tablespoon vinegar (rice or white wine)
2 tablespoons lite soy sauce
1 tablespoon sesame oil

1 teaspoon grated fresh ginger
1 large red chilli, halved,
deseeded and finely chopped
2 spring onions, finely sliced
½ cup coriander leaves

Slice the cucumber lengthways and, using a teaspoon, scoop out and discard the seeds. Slice the cucumber on the diagonal into thickish, chunky pieces. Mix with the other ingredients, tossing to coat the cucumber well with the dressing.

Homemade Sweet Chilli Sauce

For a milder chilli sauce, first remove some of the seeds from the chillies.

Makes 3 small jars, about 750 ml

2 cups bird's-eye chillies
8 cloves garlic
2 tablespoons grated fresh ginger

3 cups sugar
3 cups white vinegar

Chop the chillies and garlic roughly. Place all ingredients in a saucepan and simmer for 45–50 minutes. Purée the mixture then bring back to the boil. Pour into sterilised jars and seal. Once opened, store in the fridge.

Cook School Tip

When chopping chillies, the hottest part is the membrane around the seeds. You do not want to get any residue in your eye, or anywhere else. I always use disposable gloves when handling chillies.

Portobellos Stuffed with Cheese, Bacon and Pesto

Serves 4

4 large portobello mushrooms
4 teaspoons basil pesto
¾ cup grated mozzarella
salt and freshly ground black pepper
2 tablespoons pine nuts
2 rashers rindless streaky bacon, chopped
sprigs of parsley to garnish

Preheat the oven to 200°C. Line a grill pan or shallow roasting dish with non-stick baking paper or spray with baking spray.

Remove stalks from the mushrooms and finely chop them. Place mushrooms gill-side up in the prepared dish. Mix pesto, cheese and chopped mushroom stalks together and season as desired. Spoon into the mushrooms, and top with pine nuts and chopped bacon.

Bake for 15–20 minutes until bacon is crispy and the cheese bubbling and lightly browned. Serve garnished with sprigs of parsley.

Tofu, Kumara and Mushroom Salad

Tamari is a naturally fermented soy sauce with a mellow flavour, but you
can use regular soy sauce instead.

Serves 4

---

1 large golden kumara, peeled and cut into small cubes
1 tablespoon olive oil
½ teaspoon Mexican chilli powder
1 cup vegetable or chicken stock
2 tablespoons tamari
350 g block firm tofu, cut into cubes the same size as the kumara
2 cups sliced baby mushrooms
2 handfuls baby spinach leaves
3 tablespoons sweet chilli sauce
½ cup sliced almonds

Preheat the oven to 200°C. Toss the kumara in the olive oil and chilli powder in
a roasting dish. Bake for 30 minutes until just tender.

Heat the stock and tamari in a small saucepan. Add the tofu cubes and
mushrooms. Simmer for 10 minutes and drain, reserving the liquid.

In a salad bowl or on a platter, arrange spinach leaves. Cover with kumara,
drained tofu and mushrooms. Mix the sweet chilli sauce into the reserved liquid
and drizzle over the salad. Sprinkle with sliced almonds.

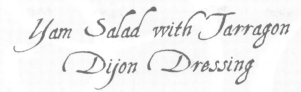

Yam Salad with Tarragon Dijon Dressing

This tasty salad can be stored for 2–3 hours in the fridge before serving.

Serves 4

For the salad
700 g scrubbed yams (any colour)
1 cup chopped parsley
3 spring onions, finely sliced (green part only)
1 tablespoon chopped fresh tarragon leaves

For the dressing
1 teaspoon caster sugar
1 tablespoon Dijon mustard
¼ cup white wine vinegar
¾ cup olive oil
2 tablespoons fresh tarragon leaves

To prepare the salad, finely slice the yams. (I use a food processor with a slicing disc.) Mix sliced yams, parsley, spring onions and tarragon in a bowl.

To make the dressing, combine all the ingredients in a screw-top jar and pour over the salad. Toss to mix the dressing through.

Carrot and Cumin Salad

This salad is best made ahead and left for the flavours to infuse.

Serves 6

———

1.5 kg small carrots, peeled, but left whole
1–2 cloves garlic, crushed (½ teaspoon)
2 teaspoons cumin seeds, toasted
2 teaspoons sesame seeds
1 tablespoon honey
1 tablespoon lemon juice
½ cup sultanas
½ cup pine nuts, toasted
2 tablespoons olive oil
1 bunch coriander leaves or flat-leafed parsley, chopped

Boil the whole carrots in lightly salted water for 8–10 minutes until just tender. They could be steamed, if preferred.

Mix the garlic, cumin and sesame seeds, honey and lemon juice. (I do this in a blender.) Drain the carrots and slice on the diagonal. Tip into a serving bowl or onto a platter. Toss with the seed mixture, sultanas, pine nuts, olive oil and chopped herbs. Serve at room temperature.

Traditional Highlander Dressing

An oldie but a goodie . . .

Makes 2 cups

———

1 x 400 g can sweetened condensed milk
1 cup malt vinegar
1 teaspoon salt
2 teaspoons dry mustard powder

Beat all ingredients together until well combined. Store in a covered container or screw-top jar in the fridge.

Clever Citrus Dressing

Makes 3 cups

———

2 cups lite oil (I use canola)
¾ cup white wine vinegar
1 tablespoon Dijon mustard
3 tablespoons chopped parsley
2 tablespoons citrus drink powder (I use Refresh)
1 teaspoon salt
freshly ground black pepper

Place all ingredients in a blender or food processor and process until well combined. Store in a covered container or screw-top jar in the fridge.

Black Sesame Dressing

Black sesame seeds are available in the Asian section of good supermarkets
or in Asian food stores. You can also use toasted sesame seeds.

Makes ¾ cup

3 tablespoons sweet chilli sauce
grated rind and juice of 2 limes
1 teaspoon sesame oil
1 teaspoon black sesame seeds

Whisk all ingredients together in a small bowl. Serve as a dressing and dipping
sauce to zing up salads and nibbles.

Aunty Rosa's Italian Dressing

Makes 3 cups

1¾ cups white wine vinegar
1 cup olive oil
grated rind and juice of 1 lemon
2–3 cloves garlic, crushed (1 teaspoon)
¼ teaspoon salt
¼ teaspoon freshly ground black pepper
½ teaspoon paprika
1 teaspoon honey
1 tablespoon finely grated Parmesan
½ teaspoon dried basil, oregano and dried dill tips

Combine all ingredients in a blender and mix well. Chill in a squeezy bottle.

Garlic and Rosemary Roasted Potatoes

Most kinds of potatoes — mashing and the new waxy varieties — can be used for this recipe. The potatoes will be nice and crisp and the garlic cloves sweet and mellow.

Serves 4

750 g potatoes, scrubbed (cut into even-sized chunks if large)
4 tablespoons olive oil
1 teaspoon garlic salt
1 whole bulb garlic, broken up into cloves (no need to peel)
2–3 small bunches rosemary, plus extra to garnish

Preheat the oven to 200°C.

Place potatoes in a roasting dish and drizzle with the olive oil. Sprinkle with garlic salt. Toss to coat evenly. Place garlic and rosemary over the potatoes. Roast for 20 minutes then give a good stir and cook for a further 15–20 minutes until crispy and golden brown.

Serve hot with the cooked rosemary removed and fresh rosemary leaves sprinkled over to garnish.

ORGANIC
ILAM HARDY
$3.00 Kg

Spicy Peach Salsa

A nice variation of this simple fresh salsa is to use a small pawpaw (papaya)
instead of the peach.

---

3 peaches, finely chopped (no need to peel)
2 tablespoons lemon juice
2 spring onions, finely chopped
3 tablespoons sweet chilli sauce
¼ cup parsley or coriander leaves
1 teaspoon olive oil

Mix all ingredients together and serve within an hour before the peach starts to
discolour.

Parsnip Fritters

Serve these tasty fritters with black sesame dressing (see page 259)
as a dipping sauce on the side.

Serves 6–8 as nibbles

2 cups peeled and grated parsnip
½ cup grated tasty cheese
2 eggs
½ teaspoon salt
freshly ground black pepper
¾ cup self-raising flour
oil to fry

Place grated parsnip in a bowl and pour a kettleful of boiling water over it. Leave for 2 minutes then drain in a sieve, squishing down to remove all excess liquid. Mix in the grated cheese, eggs, salt and pepper and self-raising flour. Mix well.

Heat a tablespoon of oil in a large non-stick frypan and fry 6 small spoonfuls of mixture at a time, pressing flat with a fish slice. Turn when golden brown and cook the other side. Keep warm as you cook the remainder of the batch. Serve with a bowl of black sesame dressing on the side.

Crispy Onion Rings

Serves 4

1 cup self-raising flour
2 eggs, separated
1 tablespoon canola or lite oil, plus extra to fry
150 ml milk
2–3 large onions, sliced into 1 cm rings
salt and freshly ground black pepper

Place flour, egg yolks, 1 tablespoon oil and milk in a food processor or blender and combine well. Whisk egg whites until stiff and fold into the batter. Dip the onion rings into batter, coating well, then fry for 3–4 minutes in oil at 190°C until golden, crispy and browned.

Drain on paper towels. Sprinkle with salt and black pepper. Serve immediately.

Grace

Grace nourishes our **souls** as we
nourish our **bodies**.

Green Coconut Rice

This makes a nice change from plain white rice.

Serves 6

———

2¾ cups long grain rice
5 cups boiling water
1 cup coconut cream
½ cup chopped fresh parsley
½ cup chopped coriander leaves
salt and freshly ground black pepper

Preheat the oven to 190°C. Wash the rice in a sieve under cold running water for 1 minute. Place rice in a large ovenproof dish, such as a casserole dish with a tight-fitting lid. Add the boiling water and coconut cream. Stir until well mixed and the rice has no lumps. Cover with the lid and bake for 30 minutes. Stir in the parsley and coriander and season as desired.

Baked Cauliflower and Broccoli Gratin

Serves 4–6

½ cauliflower, trimmed into florets
1 large head broccoli, trimmed into florets
100 g butter
½ cup flour
½ teaspoon salt
½ teaspoon freshly ground black pepper
2¼ cups milk
1 cup grated tasty cheese
½ cup finely grated Parmesan
½ cup fresh breadcrumbs (2 slices white bread
crumbed in a food processor)

Preheat the oven to 180°C. Spray a 20 cm x 30 cm lasagne or ovenproof dish with baking spray.

Bring a large saucepan of water to the boil. Add cauliflower and broccoli florets and bring back to the boil for 3 minutes until just tender. Drain and place in the prepared dish. Place butter in the saucepan and whisk as it melts. Whisk in the flour and salt and pepper. Gradually mix in the milk, whisking as you go. Continue whisking until the sauce thickens and is quite smooth.

Pour sauce over the vegetables, and sprinkle cheeses and breadcrumbs on the top. Bake for 20–25 minutes until bubbly and golden brown.

Turkish Haloumi and Couscous Fritters with Pistachio Apricot Yoghurt Sauce

You can vary this dish by using other fruit chutneys to flavour the yoghurt.

Serves 4

For the fritters
1½ cups cooked couscous
200 g Haloumi, chopped
grated rind of 2 lemons
1 cup coarsely chopped parsley
1 egg
oil for frying

For the sauce
2 cups thick, creamy natural yoghurt
½ cup apricot chutney
1–2 cloves garlic, crushed (½ teaspoon)
½ cup chopped parsley
¼ cup chopped pistachio nuts, plus a few extra to garnish

To make the fritters, combine the couscous, Haloumi, lemon rind, parsley and egg in a food processor until the mixture resembles breadcrumbs. Heat the oil in a large non-stick frypan. With wet hands, form the crumb mixture into 12 round fritters. Fry over medium heat until golden brown on both sides (you will have to do this in batches). Drain on paper towels and keep warm while you cook the remainder of the batch.

To make the sauce, mix all the ingredients together. Spoon over the warm fritters and garnish with extra pistachio nuts.

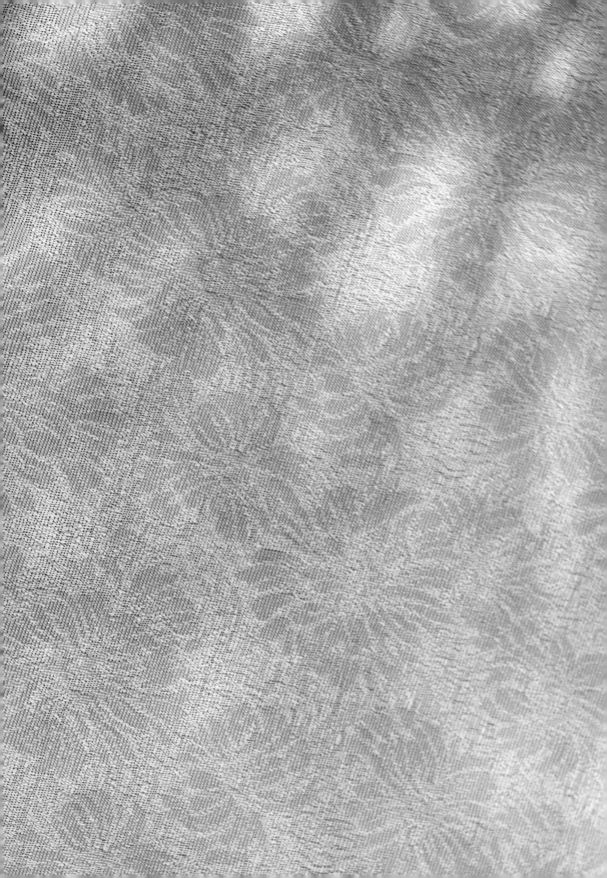

6. Scrumptious Desserts

Take the stress out of dessert and make it easy peasy so that you can enjoy the preparation as much as the occasion!

Just-like-Nana's Fresh Gooseberry Tart

Serve this tangy tart with softly whipped cream, ice cream or good old-fashioned custard.

1 sheet frozen sweet shortcrust pastry, thawed
2 cups fresh gooseberries
200 ml cream
½ cup caster sugar
3 eggs
1 tablespoon custard powder
icing sugar to dust

Preheat the oven to 180°C. Spray a 12 cm x 30 cm tart tin with baking spray.

Roll the sheet of pastry to fit the tart tin. You may need to cut and join the pastry to fit neatly. Place the pastry-lined tin in the freezer to firm up while you pick over the fresh gooseberries, topping and tailing as you go.

Place the gooseberries in the chilled pastry shell. Whisk the cream, caster sugar, eggs and custard powder together until well combined. Gently pour over the gooseberries and bake for 30–35 minutes until the pastry is golden brown and the filling is set. Dust with icing sugar to serve.

Pina Colada Cake

With only four ingredients, this cake is 'easy peasy' at its best. For an extra kick, you can replace 2 tablespoons of the pineapple juice with rum, but the icing on this cake is very definitely the icing on the cake!

For the cake
2 x 420 g cans crushed pineapple in juice
4 cups self-raising flour
1½ cups sugar
¾ cup dessicated coconut

For the frosting
100 g butter, softened to room temperature
250 g regular cream cheese, softened to room temperature
2 cups icing sugar
½ teaspoon coconut essence
toasted long-thread coconut to garnish

Preheat the oven to 180°C. Spray a 23 cm spring-form tin with baking spray and line the base with non-stick baking paper.

To make the cake, mix all ingredients together, including the juice from the pineapple, until well combined. Spoon into the prepared tin and bake for 45–50 minutes until the cake is golden and firm and pulling away from the sides of the tin. Cool in the tin.

To make the frosting, put the butter, cream cheese, icing sugar and coconut essence in a bowl and beat until smooth. Spread over the top and sides of the cooled cake and decorate with toasted coconut threads.

Smashed Toffee Apple Crumble with Caramel Toffee Sauce

Apple crumble is hard to beat on a winter's night. The toffee sauce
will keep in the fridge for 2–3 weeks.

Serves 4–6

For the toffee and sauce
1½ cups sugar
¼ cup water
200 ml cream

For the crumble
6–8 large Granny Smith apples
¾ cup brown sugar
¾ cup flour
75 g cold butter, cut into cubes
2 cups sliced almonds

To make the toffee and sauce, swirl the sugar and water in a small non-stick
saucepan and bring to the boil. Swirl as the sugar dissolves, then boil hard,
without stirring, just occasionally swirling the pan. Watch carefully for the
mixture to suddenly turn the colour of golden syrup. Remove from the heat at
this stage and wait for the bubbles to subside. Place a sheet of non-stick baking
paper on the bench. Spoon half the toffee syrup onto the paper and allow to set.
When set, break into pieces.

Add the cream to the remainder of the toffee syrup, taking care to avoid being
splashed. (It will splutter and crackle even though it will have begun to set.)
Gently stir over medium heat so that the toffee melts into the cream, producing
a smooth caramel sauce. (It will thicken as it cools.) Store in the fridge and warm
gently before serving.

To make the crumble, preheat the oven to 180°C. Spray a pie dish or small
lasagne dish with baking spray.

Peel the apples and slice into the prepared dish. Place the sugar, flour and
butter into a food processor and process to combine. Add the set toffee pieces
and the sliced almonds and pulse without overprocessing. Sprinkle this mixture
over the apple. Bake for 20–25 minutes until the apples are soft and the topping
crispy and golden brown. Serve with the warmed sauce and cream or ice cream.

Cinnamon Custard Cake

If you don't have time to make and cool the custard, you can stir the cinnamon
into store-bought custard instead.

For the custard
3 tablespoons custard powder
2 tablespoons caster sugar
1 teaspoon ground cinnamon
250 ml milk
25 g butter
2 teaspoons vanilla essence

For the cake
250 g butter
1 cup caster sugar
4 eggs
1½ cups self-raising flour
1 teaspoon ground cinnamon
¾ cup custard powder
icing sugar to dust

To make the custard, place custard powder, sugar, cinnamon and milk in a small
saucepan and stir as it comes to the boil and thickens. Remove from heat and
beat in the butter and vanilla. Cover surface with cling film and allow to cool.

Preheat the oven to 180°C. Spray a 23 cm spring-form tin with baking spray
and line the base with non-stick baking paper.

To make the cake, beat the butter and sugar until pale and creamy. Add the
eggs, one at a time, and beat well. Fold in the flour, cinnamon and custard
powder. Spread half the mixture into the tin. Carefully top with a layer of
custard then add the remaining cake mixture. This is a bit of a gooey process but
just kind of blob it in. Bake for 40–50 minutes. Cool in the tin on a wire rack.
Carefully remove from the tin when cold and dust with icing sugar to serve.

Fresh Summer Fruit in Rosewater Syrup

This fruit salad can be carried to a picnic in a wide-mouthed vacuum flask or in a plastic box wrapped in a tea towel with frozen pads to keep it deliciously cool.

Serves 6–8

100 ml water
2 tablespoons caster sugar
2 tablespoons culinary rosewater
(available in delis or the gourmet section of good supermarkets)
grated rind and juice of 2 oranges
seeds from 1 pomegranate
2 peaches, sliced
2 nectarines, sliced
1 punnet raspberries
1 punnet strawberries
½ cup blueberries
1 cup whole cherries, stones removed
fresh spray-free rose petals to garnish (optional)

Place the water and sugar in a small saucepan and heat until the sugar is dissolved. Add the rosewater and the orange rind and juice. Allow to cool. Divide the prepared fruit between 6–8 glasses or small bowls. Drizzle syrup evenly over the fruit. Serve chilled. Garnish with rose petals, if using.

Cheat's Crème Brûlée

*No one will ever know you cheated, as long as you remember to
hide the evidence!*

Serves 6–8

1 litre store-bought custard
1 cup sugar
½ cup water

Pour custard into small coffee cups or ramekins and freeze until firm, preferably
overnight.

Two hours before serving, place sugar and water in a small saucepan and swirl
around to mix. Heat, swirling the saucepan to dissolve the sugar. Bring to the
boil and watch carefully as it caramelises to a deep golden colour. Carefully pour
or spoon the caramel over the cold custard and store in the fridge until required.

The great gift of *appetite* is that there is always something new and fresh to *savour*.

Pumpkin Streusel Cheesecakes

Makes 12 individual cheesecakes

For the crust

1 cup flour
¾ cup brown sugar
100 g butter, cut into small cubes
1 cup pecan or walnut pieces
¾ cup rolled oats

For the topping

1 cup sour cream
2 tablespoons caster sugar
½ teaspoon vanilla essence

For the filling

250 g cream cheese (soft variety)
1 cup pumpkin purée
(microwave pumpkin and mash with
a fork)
½ cup sugar
1 egg
2 teaspoons ground cinnamon
1 teaspoon ground ginger

Preheat the oven to 180°C. Spray a 12-cup mini-cheesecake pan or a 23 cm square loose-bottomed cake tin with baking spray and line the base with non-stick baking paper. Line a separate sponge roll tin with non-stick baking paper.

To make the crust, place the flour, sugar and butter in a food processor and run the machine until the mixture resembles coarse breadcrumbs. Add the nuts and rolled oats and use the pulse button to just lightly incorporate, taking care to avoid cutting them too finely. Reserve ½ cup of the crust mixture and press the remainder into the base of the prepared cheesecake tin or tins. Bake for 25–30 minutes. Sprinkle the reserved mixture into the prepared sponge roll tin and bake for 10–12 minutes until crusty and golden. Set aside to cool.

To make the filling, place all the ingredients in the food processor and process until smooth. (There is no need to wash the bowl between processing the crust and cake.) Spoon the filling into the baked crust and return to the oven for 20 minutes, so the filling is lightly set. Remove the cheesecake(s) from the oven.

To make the topping, mix all ingredients together and spread over the hot filling. Bake for a further 5 minutes until the topping is set and bubbling at the edges. Sprinkle the toasted crumbs over the topping and gently press in. Cool, then chill until completely cold.

This delicious dessert is great for hassle-free entertaining, *despite the long list of ingredients. Make it up to 2 days ahead and store in the fridge. If you don't have mini-cheescake pans, make a single cheesecake in a spring-form tin.*

Macadamia and Walnut Baklava

Baklava comes from the Middle East and though it looks impressive is easy to make. Try it with cashews, almonds, pistachios or pine nuts.

Makes 16 pieces

For the baklava	For the syrup
1 cup toasted macadamias	1 cup caster sugar
1 cup walnut pieces	½ cup water
½ cup caster sugar	¼ cup honey
1 teaspoon ground cinnamon	1 tablespoon lemon juice
1 teaspoon mixed spice	grated rind of 1 lemon
1 packet (about 12 sheets) filo pastry	1 teaspoon ground cinnamon
150 g butter, melted	

Preheat the oven to 160°C. Spray a 20 cm x 30 cm sponge roll tin with baking spray.

To make the filling, chop the nuts together until they resemble coarse crumbs. Mix with the caster sugar and spices. Brush a sheet of filo with melted butter and place another on top. Brush this layer and place a third sheet on top. Place this three-layer stack into the prepared tin. Cover with one-third of the nut mixture. Repeat until you have made four three-sheet layers of filo, finishing with a pastry layer. Carefully cut diagonally into diamond shapes, using a serrated knife or scissors. Brush the surface with the remaining butter and bake for 30–35 minutes until golden brown and crisp. Turn the oven down if it is browning too quickly.

To make the syrup, place all the ingredients in a small saucepan and simmer for 10–15 minutes, then cool. As soon as you take the baklava from the oven, carefully pour the syrup over the top and leave to cool for at least 3 hours to soak up the syrup. Serve with thick, creamy Greek-style yoghurt or cream.

Cook School Tip

When using filo pastry, you need to work quickly on a dry surface and keep the filo covered to prevent it drying out. I use a lightly dampened clean tea towel.

Sticky Lime and Passionfruit Delicious

This easy-to-make and drop-dead impressive dessert has culinary star status.
It's a make-over of an old-fashioned pud — like Nana used to make. Under
the ordinary-looking sponge topping is gooey lime and passionfruit that's
hard to resist.

Serves 4

pulp of 4 passionfruit (½ cup)
75 g butter, softened
1 cup caster sugar
grated rind of 3 limes
4 eggs, separated
½ cup flour
300 ml milk
100 ml fresh lime juice
icing sugar to dust
edible gold dust (available from cake-decorating shops, optional)

Preheat the oven to 175°C. Spray four ¾ cup ramekins or small bowls with
baking spray.

Divide the passionfruit pulp between the prepared ramekins. Place ramekins
in a roasting dish. Beat the butter, sugar and lime rind together until pale. Add
the egg yolks, one at a time, and continue beating as you add the flour, milk and
lime juice. (Sometimes the mixture looks quite curdled. Don't worry — that will
change as it cooks.)

Put the jug on now. In a separate metal, glass or china bowl beat the egg
whites until they form soft, floppy peaks. Fold these into the other mixture then
quickly divide between the ramekins. Pour boiling water into the roasting dish
so that it comes three-quarters of the way up the sides of the ramekins.

Carefully place the dish in the oven and bake for 20–25 minutes. The sponge
topping should be pale, risen and firm to touch. Serve warm dusted with icing
sugar and edible gold dust, if using, with soft whipped cream or ice cream on
the side.

Dark Chocolate Sorbet

This is a fabulous velvety dessert that really isn't so bad for you — and just
a little portion is deliciously satisfying. It's wonderful with the last few
sips of red wine.

Serves 4

1 cup caster sugar
500 ml water
200 g best quality dark chocolate

In a small saucepan, stir the sugar and water over gentle heat until the sugar is
dissolved. Cool to room temperature. Melt the chocolate either in a bowl over a
saucepan of simmering water or in the microwave. Stir until smooth and cool to
room temperature.

Place both cooled mixtures together and churn in an ice-cream machine until
frozen. Scoop into a plastic container and store in the freezer. Allow to soften
out of the freezer for a few minutes before scooping into small glasses or dishes
to serve.

Cook School Tips for Melting Chocolate

Melting chocolate can sometimes be a little bit fiddly as it is heat
sensitive and can scorch, turning it into a lumpy mess. If chocolate
gets to this stage it cannot be saved. You will need to start again.
If you follow these guidelines all should be well:

1 Break it into small, even pieces and place in a glass or ceramic bowl.

2 Place the bowl over a saucepan of water, making sure it is a tight fit.

3 Simmer the water on low to avoid condensation getting into the chocolate.

4 Use a metal spoon to stir the chocolate.

5 Remove the chocolate from the heat when there are still tiny little lumps in
   the molten chocolate. (The bowl will remain warm enough to complete the
   melting process.)

• Alternatively, if you want to use a microwave to melt chocolate, first cut it
   into small pieces. Place in an uncovered microwaveproof bowl and microwave
   at 50 per cent power in 1 minute bursts, stirring after every minute.

Baby Hazelnut Sweetiepies

This is a version of my famous baby pecan pies. This one uses hazelnuts, which grow very well here in Oxford, and hazelnut spread, which is more commonly known as Nutella.

Makes 16

For the pastry
125 g butter
1 cup flour
½ cup icing sugar

For the filling
1 cup hazelnuts, skins removed and chopped
8 teaspoons Nutella
60 g butter
1 egg
1 cup brown sugar
½ teaspoon hazelnut or
vanilla essence

Spray 16 cups of a 24-cup mini-muffin tin with baking spray.

To make the pastry, place all the ingredients into a food processor and run the machine until the pastry clumps around the blade. Divide pastry into 16 small balls and, using floured hands, press each ball into the base and up the sides of a cup of the prepared mini-muffin tin. Place tin in the freezer to chill for 15–20 minutes until the pastry is really firm and hard.

Preheat the oven to 180°C. For the filling, divide the chopped nuts between the pastry-lined cups, then place a ½ teaspoon of Nutella on top of each sprinkling of nuts. Melt the butter in a small bowl. Whisk in the egg, sugar and essence until smooth, but somewhat gluey. Using a small jug, pour 1 teaspoon of mixture into each nut-filled cup and bake for 20–25 minutes until the pastry is golden brown and the filling set and crisp.

Remove from the oven and cool for 5 minutes in the tins, until the pies are cool enough to handle. Give each pie a little twist to loosen the bottom, then carefully lift out to cool completely on a wire rack.

The filling makes enough for a couple of batches, but it is best not to double the pastry ingredients. Instead, make a second batch straight after the first.

Lemony Apple Tart

You need to be prepared to make this dessert to allow time to chill the pastry — this will relax the gluten molecules in the flour and prevent the pastry from shrinking from the sides of the tin and rising in the middle when baked.

For the pastry
1 cup flour
⅓ cup self-raising flour
150 g butter, cold
2 egg yolks
3–4 tablespoons cold water

For the filling
2 eggs
grated rind and juice of 1 lemon
1 cup sugar
2 tablespoons butter, melted
3 large Braeburn or Granny Smith
apples, grated (no need to peel)
icing sugar to dust

To make the pastry, place the flours and butter into a food processor and run the machine until the mixture resembles breadcrumbs. Add the egg yolks, just pulsing the machine to combine. Dribble in the water while pulsing the machine, until the mixture clumps together in a ball. Gather the dough and press into a flat plate shape then wrap in cling film and chill in the fridge for 30 minutes.

Preheat the oven to 200°C. Spray a 23–25 cm fluted pie dish with baking spray.

Roll the pastry out on a lightly floured surface and line the pie dish. Place the pastry-lined tin in the fridge or freezer for a few minutes.

To make the filling, combine the eggs, lemon rind and juice, sugar and melted butter. Pour into the chilled pastry shell. Cover with the grated apple and bake for 10 minutes, then reduce the temperature to 160°C and bake for a further 40–45 minutes until golden brown, the pastry is pulling away from the edges and the filling has set. Serve warm, dusted with icing sugar.

Moccacino Self-saucing Pud

This recipe is easily adapted to become gluten free. Just use a good
gluten-free flour mix.

¼ cup milk

50 g butter, melted

1 egg

½ cup flour

2 teaspoons baking powder

2 tablespoons sweetened coffee and chicory essence

¼ cup ground almonds

½ cup white sugar

½ cup brown sugar

2 tablespoons cocoa

1 cup boiling water

Preheat the oven to 180°C. Spray a 4 cup or 1 litre lasagne or pie dish with
baking spray.

Beat the milk, butter and egg together then add the flour, baking powder,
coffee essence, ground almonds and white sugar. Mix well.

In a separate bowl, mix the brown sugar, cocoa and boiling water. Pour this
mixture into the base of the prepared dish. Carefully pour the pudding mixture
over this and bake for 25–35 minutes until firm and risen. Serve warm with
vanilla ice cream or softly whipped cream.

Tamarillo Brown Sugar Pie

This is a family favourite for the tamarillo season.

3 sheets frozen sweet shortcrust pastry, thawed
1 cup long-thread coconut
10–12 tamarillos
½ cup brown sugar
icing sugar to dust

Preheat the oven to 180°C. Spray a loose-bottomed deep quiche tin with baking spray.

Press the pastry into the base and up the sides of the prepared tin. (You may need to join sheets to fit.) Sprinkle half the coconut over the base and chill the pastry in the freezer.

Boil the kettle and pour boiling water over the tamarillos. Leave for 1 minute, then carefully peel off the skins and remove the stalks. Cut in half and place in the now chilled pastry base, cut-side up.

Sprinkle the remainder of the coconut and the brown sugar over the top. Cover with a sheet of pastry, crimping the edges to seal, and make a few snips in the surface to allow steam to escape.

Bake for 40–45 minutes until the pastry is nice and golden. Dust with icing sugar and serve with softly whipped cream or ice cream.

Rhubarb Ginger Fool

Any fool can make a fool. After all, it is simply stewed fruit and cream folded together. You can use this simple recipe with all sorts of cooked fruit instead of rhubarb. It's a great way to use up those slightly bruised strawberries or raspberries.

Serves 6

1 kg rhubarb stalks, trimmed and cut into 2 cm pieces
1–1½ cups sugar, to taste
½ cup finely chopped crystallised ginger
1 tablespoon grated fresh ginger
500 ml cream

Combine the rhubarb, sugar, crystallised and fresh ginger in a medium-sized saucepan with a tight-fitting lid. There is no need to add any liquid as the rhubarb will release its juices. Gently cook over medium heat for 20–25 minutes until the rhubarb is very tender and falling apart. Cool then refrigerate until very cold.

Whip the cream until it holds soft peaks. Add the rhubarb and gently fold through. Spoon into parfait glasses and keep in the fridge until ready to serve.

Vanilla-poached Peaches with Peach Ice Cream

This simple dessert can also be made with nectarines, plums or apricots.

Serves 6

For the poached peaches
6 large ripe peaches
500 ml sweet white wine
3 tablespoons clear, pourable honey
1 vanilla pod, split in half

For the peach ice cream (makes 1 litre)
2 cups stewed or canned peaches, finely
chopped or puréed in a blender
300 ml cream
1 cup vanilla custard
1 cup full cream milk

To poach the fruit, place ice cubes in a large bowl of cold water and place the peaches in another large bowl. Heat a saucepan of water or boil the kettle and pour the boiling water over the peaches. Leave for 1 minute then, using a slotted spoon, carefully lift the peaches out of the boiling water and transfer to the iced water. The skins should peel off easily.

Place the white wine, honey and vanilla pod in a saucepan large enough to hold all six peaches. Stir over gentle heat until the honey is dissolved, then add the peaches and cover. Simmer for 20 minutes, turning the fruit carefully every 5 minutes or so. Carefully lift out the softened peaches and bring the syrup to a boil, cooking until it is reduced by half. This will take about 10–15 minutes. Remove the vanilla pod. Pour syrup over the peaches and chill, covered, in the fridge. Allow to come to room temperature before serving.

To make the ice cream, combine all the ingredients and freeze in an ice-cream machine, following the manufacturer's instructions. Serve with poached peaches.

Cook School Tip

The vanilla pod will still have enough flavour to make vanilla sugar. Rinse and dry it, and store in caster sugar.

White Chocolate Mousse

This mousse needs to be chilled in the fridge for at least 4 hours before serving.

Serves 6

3 tablespoons cold water
2 teaspoons gelatine
1½ cups chopped white chocolate or white chocolate buttons
300 ml cream
fruit to garnish
white chocolate shards to garnish

Place the water in a small bowl and sprinkle the gelatine over. Let it stand without stirring, so the gelatine can absorb all the water.

Place the chocolate and cream in a small saucepan and stir over medium to high heat until the chocolate is fully melted and incorporated. Add the gelatine mixture and stir as this completely melts and dissolves. Whisk with an electric mixer for about 5 minutes until cool.

Pour into six shot glasses, espresso cups or small serving bowls (less than 1 cup capacity). Serve garnished with fruit and white chocolate shards.

This is *a sneaky idea* that uses everybody's favourite pav ingredients.

Pav in a Glass

Serves 6

300 ml cream, softly whipped
6 large or 12 small meringues, roughly crushed
1 punnet strawberries, sliced
3 kiwifruit, peeled and sliced
pulp of 6 passionfruit
mint sprigs to garnish

Layer the cream, crushed meringue pieces and fruit in six tall glasses. Garnish with mint sprigs. Keep chilled and serve with a parfait spoon.

Perfect Meringues

This recipe produces perfect meringues: crunchy outside, meltingly soft inside. The trick is to add the sugar slowly so it dissolves into the egg white.

Makes 36–40

6 egg whites (at room temperature)
2 cups caster sugar
1 teaspoon vanilla essence

1 teaspoon vinegar
2 teaspoons cornflour
whipped cream to serve

Preheat the oven to 120°C. Line a baking tray with non-stick baking paper.

In a large bowl (not plastic), beat egg whites until soft peaks form. Add the sugar, a teaspoon at a time. The mixture should get glossy, thick and shiny with each addition and the sugar-adding should take at least 10 minutes. Beat in the vanilla, vinegar and cornflour. Spoon mixture into blobs on the prepared tray. Bake for approximately 45 minutes until dry and crisp. The meringues should lift off the paper easily. Cool on a wire rack and sandwich with whipped cream.

7. Gorgeous Treats for Coffee

A tiny mouthful of something fabulous is often all that is required to satisfy the craving for a sweet ending. I often serve little shot glasses, liqueur glasses or espresso cups of a delicious morsel that can be eaten with a dinky wee coffee spoon. They're always a hit!

Ginger, Walnut and White Chocolate Fudge

Makes about 60 pieces

1 cup chopped crystallised ginger
1 cup fresh walnut pieces
2 x 400 g cans sweetened condensed milk
2 cups firmly packed soft brown sugar
250 g butter
100 ml liquid glucose syrup
(available at delis, good supermarkets and pharmacies)
3 tablespoons golden syrup
400 g white (or milk or dark) chocolate, chopped
1 teaspoon vanilla essence

Spray a 20 cm x 30 cm x 4 cm deep sponge roll tin with baking spray and line with non-stick baking paper. Sprinkle the ginger and walnuts evenly over the base of the prepared tray.

Place the sweetened condensed milk, sugar, butter and syrups in a large, heavy-based saucepan and stir over medium heat until the butter melts and the sugar dissolves. Boil gently for approximately 6–8 minutes until it reaches 116°C and changes colour to a dark caramel brown. Stir often to prevent it catching on the bottom. Remove from heat and let stand until the bubbles subside. Stir in the chocolate and vanilla and continue stirring until melted and smooth.

Pour the fudge over the ginger and nuts and smooth the surface. Cool to room temperature (about 3 hours), then put in the fridge to set. Cut into squares. It will keep in an airtight container in the fridge for up to 6 weeks — if you're lucky.

See Fabulous Fudge Inspirations and Cook School Tips over the page

Jo's Fabulous Fudge Inspirations

This is a version of Jo's Fabulous Fudge from Jo Seagar Cooks *and* **it's the best fudge you can possibly imagine**. It has the added bonus of big chunks of ginger and walnuts.

Jo's Fabulous Fudge Inspirations

You can make many versions of the fudge in this book. Always put any solid extras in the base of the paper-lined tin and carefully pour the fudge over the top — don't stir them through the liquid fudge in the saucepan — but add liquids to the fudge mixture.

Try versions with:

- any form of essence or alcohol instead of, or as well as, vanilla
- dark, milk or white chocolate: swirl together two types for a marbled look
- rum and raisins
- apricots, macadamias and Grand Marnier
- dark chocolate with smashed candy canes
- gummy sweets
- pieces of Turkish delight
- Jaffas or Crunchie bars
- or, cut into tiny heart-shapes or dip in chocolate for total decadence

---

Cook Scool Tips for Fabulous Fudge

- *Stick to well-known brands for tinned condensed milk. They are more consistent and provide a better result.*
- *Liquid glucose stops sugar from crystallising, which is what all melted sugar naturally wants to do. You need 100 ml for this recipe, but it is pretty sticky, so don't stress about making sure the measurement is exact. The recipe is fairly forgiving in that regard.*
- *Make sure you use a heavy non-stick saucepan for the fudge.*
- *The best thing to stir fudge with is a silicone spatula because it won't melt. When shopping for this can't-live-without utensil, get one with a wooden, metal or silicone handle.*
- *Use a sugar thermometer to take the guesswork out of cooking fudge. As soon as it reaches 116°C it will set. It sits at 110°C for a while, so you really have to watch it and take it off the heat the moment it hits 116°C. It won't set at lower temperatures.*

Homemade fudge is pure indulgence.
Unless you have the willpower of a saint, make it
when you are expecting a crowd or planning to
give it away. Otherwise you may need to check the
fridge on a regular basis to make sure it's still there!

Mint Truffles

Makes 40

2 x 200 g packets Mint Slice biscuits
250 g regular cream cheese
½ cup icing sugar
375 g dark chocolate melts (1 packet)

Place the biscuits in a food processor and run the machine to crush them. Add the cream cheese and mix well. It does not matter if there are bits of biscuit still intact.

Line a tray with non-stick baking paper. Spoon out little balls of mixture, rolling in icing sugar to prevent the mixture sticking to your hands. (This is quite a messy process.) Place balls in the freezer for an hour.

Melt the chocolate in a microwave or over a bowl of simmering water. Using a fork, dip each frozen truffle in chocolate and allow to set on a sheet of non-stick baking paper. Store in an airtight container in a cool, dark place. To prevent the chocolate sweating, do not store in the fridge or freezer.

Apricot and Tangelo Fruit Log

I like to use dried apricots from Otago — the flavour is superb.

Makes 2 logs or 20 pieces

2 cups dried apricots, chopped
grated rind of 1 large tangelo
½ teaspoon citric acid
¾ cup icing sugar
1 cup ground almonds
1 cup desiccated coconut, plus 1 cup to roll the logs in

Place all ingredients except the extra coconut in a food processor and run the machine to form a sticky paste. Scrape out and form into two logs. Roll them in the extra coconut and wrap in cling film.

Chill in the freezer for at least an hour before slicing each log diagonally into 10 pieces. Keep in the fridge and serve chilled as the mixture is quite soft at room temperature.

Cranberry White Chocolate Truffles

**If you want a gift that will wow everyone at Christmas time or for a special
Valentine then look no further than this recipe.**

Makes 55–60 truffles

2 cups dried cranberries (Craisins)
½ cup Cointreau, Grand Marnier or freshly squeezed orange juice
100 g butter
750 g white chocolate melts (2 packets)
2½ cups icing sugar
gold foil truffle cases (optional)

Place dried cranberries and liqueur or juice in a microwaveproof jug, cook on
high for 3–4 minutes and set aside to cool. The cranberries will absorb the liquid
and plump up. Add the butter and 375 g white chocolate melts (1 packet)
and microwave again in bursts of 30 seconds, stirring after each burst, until
the chocolate has melted. Stir in the icing sugar and allow the mixture to cool
enough to handle. Roll into small balls the size of large marbles. Place these on a
plastic tray and freeze for at least an hour until solid.

Place the second 375 g of melts in a small metal bowl over a saucepan of hot
water and gently melt until smooth. Using a fork, dip each frozen truffle in
white chocolate and allow to set on a sheet of non-stick baking paper. Then place
in gold foil truffle cases, if using. Store in an airtight container in a cool, dark
place. To prevent the chocolate sweating, do not store in the fridge or freezer.

Whisky Truffles

Makes 25–30

750 g dark chocolate melts (2 packets)
½ cup cream
2 tablespoons whisky

Place 375 g melts (1 packet), cream and whisky in a small saucepan and stir gently over very low heat as the chocolate melts. Stir until smoothly combined then cool and chill in the fridge. Roll into small balls the size of large marbles. (I find using two teaspoons is the easiest way of doing this.) Place these on a plastic tray and freeze for at least an hour until solid.

Place the second 375 g of melts in a small metal bowl over a saucepan of hot water and gently melt until smooth. Using a fork, dip each frozen truffle in chocolate and allow to set on a sheet of non-stick baking paper. Store in an airtight container in a cool, dark place. To prevent the chocolate sweating, do not store in the fridge or freezer.

Lime and White Chocolate Rocky Road

Makes 48 pieces

250 g white chocolate bits
2 cups blanched almonds, chopped
2 cups white marshmallows, cut in half
1 cup long-thread coconut
grated rind of 3 small limes
1 x 300 g block white nougat, chopped
(or 4 x 75 g Damascus French Nougat bars, chopped)
750 g white chocolate melts

Spray a 20 x 30 cm sponge roll tin with baking spray and line with non-stick baking paper.

Place the white chocolate bits, chopped almonds, marshmallow pieces, coconut, lime rind and chopped nougat in a bowl. Mix well. Gently melt the white chocolate melts in the microwave or over a bowl of simmering water. Pour into the other ingredients and mix well, then pour into the prepared tin. Set in the fridge for at least 3 hours. When set firm, lift out and cut into pieces. Store in an airtight container in the fridge.

Kahlúa Macadamia Chocolate Fudge

Forget the mid-afternoon coffee to perk you up! One piece of this will give you that sweet coffee effect in one scrumptious hit.

Makes 25–30 pieces

1 x 400 g can sweetened condensed milk
¼ cup Kahlúa liqueur
2 tablespoons instant coffee granules
2 cups chocolate chips
1 cup chopped macadamia nuts

Line a 20 cm square cake tin with non-stick baking paper.

Place condensed milk, Kahlúa and coffee granules in a saucepan over medium heat. Stir and bring the mixture to a simmer. Cook for about 3 minutes, stirring constantly until the coffee granules melt and the mixture thickens. Remove from heat and stir in the chocolate chips, stirring until melted. Stir in the nuts and pour into the prepared tin. Refrigerate for at least 2 hours, but preferably overnight. Lift out of the tin and cut into squares.

Florentine Nuggets

Makes 60 bite-sized pieces

400 g dark chocolate
1 cup cornflakes
1 cup currants
2 cups flaked almonds
2 cups glacé cherries, cut in half
1 cup mixed peel
1 x 400 g can sweetened condensed milk

Preheat the oven to 180°C. Spray a 20 cm x 30 cm sponge roll tin with baking spray and line with non-stick baking paper.

Melt the chocolate in the microwave or over a saucepan of simmering water and spread evenly over the base of the prepared tin. Refrigerate to set.

Put the cornflakes, currants, flaked almonds, cherries, mixed peel and condensed milk in a large bowl. Mix well with a spatula then spread over the chocolate base. Bake for 12–15 minutes until golden brown. Cool in the tin then chill. Cut into bite-sized squares just before serving.

Rose Turkish Delight

Makes 60 pieces

4 cups sugar
4½ cups boiling water
1 tablespoon citric acid
1 cup cornflour, plus 2 tablespoons
1 teaspoon cream of tartar
1 tablespoon culinary rosewater (available in delis
or the gourmet section of good supermarkets)
1–2 drops pink food colouring
3 tablespoons icing sugar

Line a 20 cm x 20 cm square cake tin with tinfoil and spray with baking spray. Place sugar, 1½ cups boiling water and citric acid in a small heavy non-stick saucepan. Stir until sugar dissolves and bring the mixture to the boil. Boil gently, without stirring, just swirling the saucepan around occasionally until the mixture reaches the soft-ball stage (116°C).

Whisk the cornflour, cream of tartar and remaining 3 cups of boiling water together in a medium-sized heavy non-stick saucepan. Slowly add the sugar syrup to this mixture, whisking constantly to avoid lumps forming. Gently, while you continue stirring, bring to a simmer and cook for a further 30–40 minutes until it is pale golden in colour and very thick. Stir in the rosewater and food colouring. Pour into the prepared tin and cool, then set in the fridge overnight.

Sift the icing sugar and second measure of cornflour together. Turn the Turkish delight out of the tin and cut into 2 cm cubes. Roll in the icing sugar and cornflour. Store in an airtight container for up to 2 weeks. Separate layers with sheets of non-stick baking paper.

Cook School Tips for Making Jelly

If you want to make jelly, you can either use leaf or powdered gelatine. Leaf gelatine is nicer to work with but more difficult to find. (One leaf is equal to one level teaspoon of gelatine powder.) Follow these guidelines for best results every time:

- To make a light, wobbly jelly the ratio is 3 leaves or 3 teaspoons of powder to 600 ml of liquid.

- If you want a firm jelly, increase the gelatine to four leaves or 4 teaspoons to 600 ml of liquid.

- To use leaf gelatine, soak the leaves in iced water for at least 5 minutes until soft. Take the leaf out of the water and squeeze lightly to drain. It is now ready to be dissolved in hot liquid.

- To use powdered gelatine, sprinkle the powder over cold liquid and leave until the gelatine has soaked up all the liquid. Put in a bowl of just-simmering liquid and stir to dissolve.

Kindness

Kindness *is difficult to give away because it just keeps coming back to you.*

Cinnamon Palmiers

Makes 35–40

1 x 400 g packet frozen flaky pastry, thawed
¼ cup caster sugar
1 tablespoon ground cinnamon
1 egg, whisked

Preheat the oven to 200°C. Line two oven trays with non-stick baking paper or silicone baking sheets.

Roll out the block of pastry to make a 25 cm x 35 cm sheet. Mix the caster sugar and cinnamon together. Reserve 2 teaspoons of this and set it aside. Sprinkle the rest over the pastry.

Roll both long sides of the pastry inwards to the middle so that they meet in the centre. Fold in half lengthways to make a long log shape. Cut into 1 cm slices and lay flat on the prepared trays. Don't worry if the shape goes a bit wonky and loose, they puff up when they bake. Lightly brush the palmiers with the egg then sprinkle with the reserved cinnamon sugar. Bake for 18–20 minutes until puffed and lightly golden. Cool on a wire rack and serve warm. These can be stored in an airtight container for a couple of days but are nicest if served fresh.

Toasted Coconut Marshmallows

Makes 40

4 tablespoons gelatine
¾ cup boiling water
3 cups sugar
300 ml liquid glucose
1 cup cold water
¾ cup finely dessicated coconut
1 teaspoon coconut essence
1¾ cups icing sugar
4 tablespoons cornflour
1 cup toasted coconut (optional)

Line a 20 cm x 30 cm sponge roll tin with tinfoil and spray with baking spray.

Place gelatine and boiling water in the bowl of an electric mixer and run the machine to mix well. Allow to rest and partially set.

Boil the sugar, liquid glucose and cold water in a heavy saucepan until it reaches the soft-ball stage (116°C). Remove from heat and pour carefully over the gelatine. Turn on the mixer and beat until fluffy and very thick. Slow the mixer speed and add the coconut and coconut essence. Pour into the prepared tin and refrigerate until set.

Sift the icing sugar and cornflour together onto a sheet of baking paper or silicone. Cut marshmallows into big cubes (about 3 cm — I find that cutting with wet kitchen scissors is the easiest way) and roll in the icing sugar and cornflour mixture or toasted coconut.

Pecan Lace Biscuits with Orange Buttercream Filling

Makes 18–20 pairs

For the biscuits
100 g butter
½ cup caster sugar
3 tablespoons liquid glucose
½ cup flour
1 cup coarsely chopped pecan nuts
1 teaspoon vanilla essence

For the orange buttercream
1½ cups icing sugar
100 g butter, softened but not melted
1 teaspoon grated orange rind
4 teaspoons orange juice

Preheat the oven to 180°C. Line two oven trays with non-stick baking paper or silicone baking sheets.

To make the biscuits, place butter, sugar and liquid glucose in a medium-sized saucepan and stir as it comes to the boil. Remove from heat and stir in the flour, nuts and vanilla. Drop mixture in teaspoonfuls onto the prepared trays. Leave 6–7 cm around each biscuit for the mixture to spread. Bake one tray at a time for 10–12 minutes, until bubbling and lightly golden. Cool biscuits on the tray at least 10 minutes before carefully lifting off to cool completely on a wire rack.

To make the filling, beat all ingredients to form a fluffy frosting consistency, adding extra icing sugar or juice as needed to achieve the right consistency.

Spread a teaspoonful of butter cream mixture onto a cold biscuit and gently press another on top. Repeat with remaining biscuits. These can be stored in an airtight container in a cool, dark place for 2–3 days.

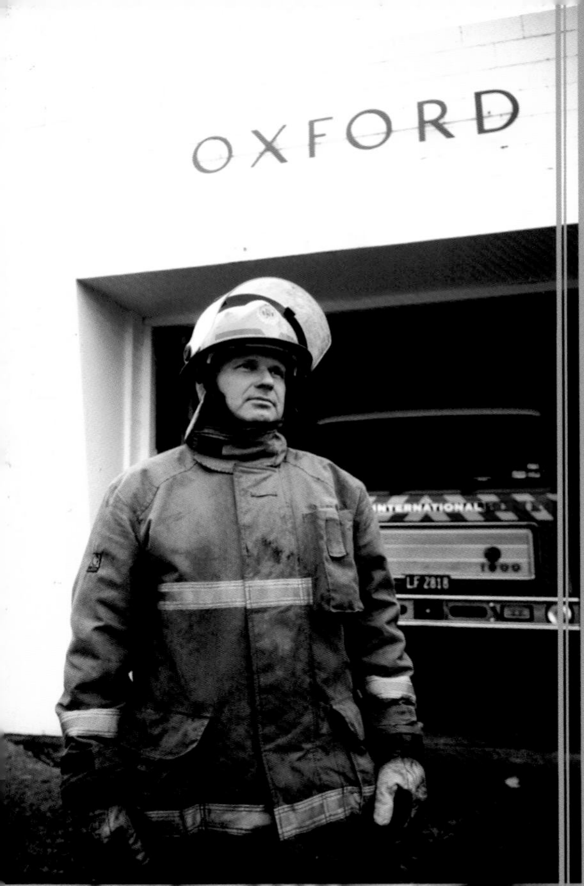
OXFORD
INTERNATIONAL
LF 2818

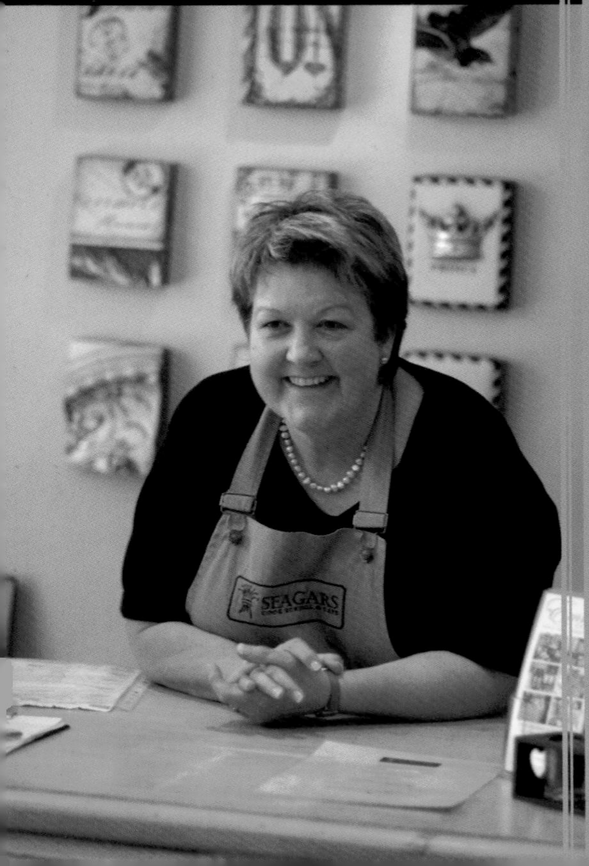
SEAGARS

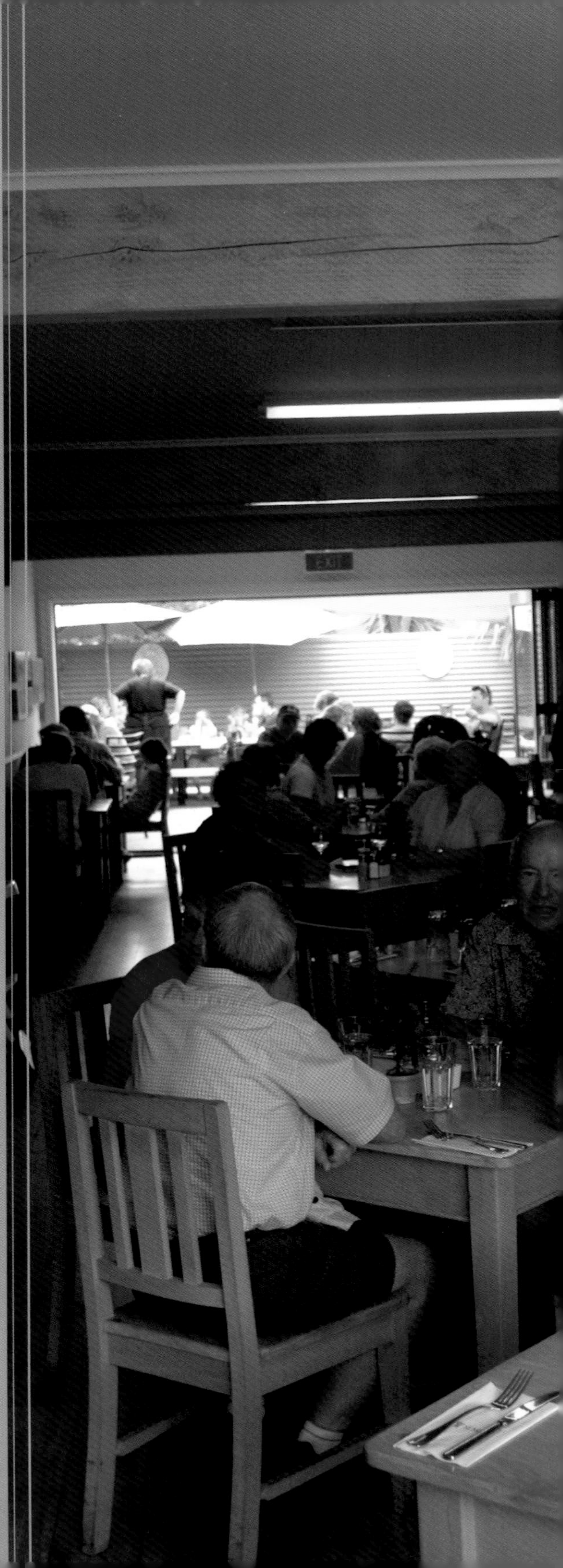
EXIT

Welcome To
The Simple Life

Essential Weights and Measures

**Working out the different wordings and quantities in recipes can become
a bit of a minefield. Here is a useful list of conversions.**

Temperature Conversions

Description	Celsius	Fahrenheit
Cool oven	110°C	225°F
Very low oven	150°C	300°F
Moderate oven	180°C	350°F
Hot oven	220°C	425°F
Very hot oven	230°C	450°F

Liquid Conversions

5 ml	1 teaspoon
15 ml	1 tablespoon
250 ml	1 cup
600 ml	1 pint
1000 ml	1 litre

NB: The Australian metric tablespoon measures 20 ml.

Length Conversions

2.5 cm	1 inch
12 cm	4½ inches
20 cm	8 inches
24 cm	9½ inches
30 cm	12 inches

Ingredients

butter	100 g	1 American stick
	225 g	1 cup
	30 g	2 tablespoons
cheese	115 g	1 cup grated tasty
	150 g	1 cup grated Parmesan
egg whites	1 large (size 8) egg white	55 ml or 30 g
flour	150 g	1 cup
golden syrup and honey	350 g	1 cup
onions	1 cup chopped	115 g
rice	200 g	1 cup uncooked rice
	165 g	1 cup cooked rice
sugar	225 g	1 cup caster or granulated sugar
	200 g	1 cup brown sugar
	125 g	1 cup icing sugar

Ingredients' Common Names

aubergine	eggplant
baking paper	parchment paper, silicone paper
cannellini beans	white kidney beans
capsicums	bell peppers
coriander	cilantro
courgette	zucchini
spring onions	green onions, scallions
fillet (of meat)	tenderloin
icing sugar	confectioners sugar
rocket	arugula, rocquette

Food Label Secrets

Understanding and interpreting food labels is another challenge altogether. Here's a list of key points to help you understand what's in the ready-made food you are buying:

- Ingredients are listed in order of volume from largest to smallest. If the first ingredient is cream, for example, you know that is the main ingredient. A short list usually means the item has fewer artificial ingredients.

- Check out the information about serving size — even quite small packages can have more than one serving.

- To get a quick idea of whether the item is a healthy choice, use the following percentage guidelines per 100 g:

  - more than 10 g of sugar is a lot and a less than 2 g is a low-sugar product
  - more than 20 g of fat is high and less than 3 g is low
  - 5 g of saturated fat is high and less than 1 g is low
  - more than 3 g of fibre is high and less than 0.5 g is low
  - more than 0.5 g of sodium is high and less than 0.1 g is low.

Acknowledgements

Thank you to the following for the loan of props for this book:
Frogmore, 70 Victoria Street, Christchurch, Canterbury
Asko Design, 76 Victoria Street, Christchurch, Canterbury
The Homestore, Merivale Mall, 189 Papanui Road, Christchurch,
Canterbury, www.thehomestorechristchurch.co.nz
Nest, www.nest.co.nz
Station Road Lifestyle and Living, 15 Coronation St, Southbrook, Canterbury
Rose and Bruce Anderson, Oxford, Canterbury
Roger Brown and the Oxford Museum, 15 Main Street, Oxford, Canterbury
Richard and Dawn Sparks at Northbrook Colonial Museum, Spark Lane,
Rangiora, Canterbury

Index